MULTICULTURAL EDUCAT

Education in a Multicultural Society

Series Editor: Maurice Craft
Professor of Education
University of Nottingham

Multicultural Education in White Schools

Sally Tomlinson

B. T. Batsford Ltd
London

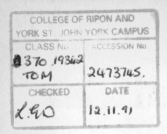
Typeset by Deltatype Ltd, Ellesmere Port, Cheshire
and printed in Great Britain by
Dotesios Printers Ltd, Trowbridge

Published by B. T. Batsford Ltd
4 Fitzhardinge Street, London W1H 0AH

A CIP catalogue record for this book is
available from the British Library

ISBN 0 7134 5786 4

Contents

Acknowledgements

I would like to thank Wigan Local Education Authority for the part-time secondment of Peter Coulson to carry out the bulk of the visits reported in Chapter 6 of this book, and to record my thanks to Peter for working so hard, and so efficiently. Also thanks to Howard Valentine, Wigan Senior Advisor, and HMI John Singh and Sinclair Rogers for helpful discussion. Thanks to the following colleagues for helpful exchanges of ideas: Clare Brown, Chris Gaine, Harry Goulbourne, Sam Sharma and Bill Taylor. Grateful thanks to my husband Brian for word-processing the book, and final thanks to all the project workers who gave up time to talk to us and share their enthusiasm and ideas for creating a decent education for all.

Sally Tomlinson
Lancaster, January 1989

Introduction

We are not looking for the assimilation of minority communities into an unchanged dominant way of life: we are perhaps looking for the 'assimilation' of *all* groups within a redefined concept of what it means to live in British society.

(Swann Report, DES, 1985a, p. 8)

As Britain moves into the 1990s the education system is becoming increasingly important in determining the relations between ethnic minorities and the white majority society. Crucial educational questions relate to whether and how education can help resolve some of the tensions and conflicts, largely a product of a period of colonial imperialism, between groups who perceive each other to be ethnically, racially or culturally different, and how to help all young people growing up in British society to understand the interdependence of individuals, groups and nations.

Since the publication of the Swann Report (DES, 1985a) the focus of multicultural education has moved from issues concerned with the education of ethnic minority pupils, to issues concerning the education of *all* pupils in an ethnically diverse society, in which acceptance of all groups as part of the British nation is becoming socially, politically and economically more important. How to offer an appropriate and relevant education to young white people, so that they will leave school able to accept that their non-white fellow-pupils are their equal fellow-citizens with equal rights and responsibilities, is becoming recognized as a serious question worthy of serious debate.

The focus of this book is on those areas of Britain which do not have substantial numbers of non-white minorities – areas described variously as monocultural regions (Taylor, 1984), non-contact areas (Taylor, 1986) and the white Highlands (Brown, 1989a) – although the reactions of white pupils and parents in areas of ethnic minority settlement is also a consideration. The book is intended as a contribution to the literature for those practitioners developing multicultural policies and practices in white areas. It aims to discuss levels of acceptance of, and resistance to, the idea that Britain is a multicultural society, and that education should reflect this; it also describes some new initiatives developing from Education Support Grant (ESG) projects in white areas, and suggests how educational developments since the 1988 Education Act may affect multicultural 'education for all'.

Despite the reference to 'white' areas, it is now difficult to locate any area of Britain that is completely 'white'. Even Cumbria, often quoted as an archetypal 'white' area, recorded over 2000 people of New Commonwealth origin in the 1981 census and Cumbria's curriculum guidelines on education for life in a multicultural society note that 'Britain has always been a multicultural society; within Cumbria itself there are groups of people very different from each other in lifestyles and attitudes' (Cumbria, 1987). Up to the mid-1980s, the limited educational research carried out in all-white areas suggested that what is now central government policy – that all pupils should be appropriately educated for life in a multi-ethnic society – had impinged only marginally on the policies and practices of local education authorities (LEAs) and schools with few or no ethnic minority pupils. Many such schools still regarded issues of ethnic and cultural diversity, multicultural education, race and racism, and wider global understandings as remote or irrelevant to their curriculum, and the idea that they should actively consider the issues and make curriculum and other changes, as being unacceptable or unnecessary.

In the later 1980s however, evidence is slowly beginning to accumulate showing that LEAs and schools in white areas are beginning to consider the issues, produce policies, and support curriculum initiatives and changed practices. There is as yet no large-scale research to provide evidence of the extent of change, and there is limited agreement and some confusion as to how to develop multicultural, non-racist and global curriculum approaches, but a good deal seems to have been accomplished in a very short period, particularly from 1984. There is now a more widespread realization that unless the whole institution of education takes a positive lead in combating cultural ignorance, ethnocentric attitudes, and racism, another generation of ignorant and racist young white people could be produced. What is needed is to develop a curriculum that reflects and develops an accurate understanding of British society and Britain's role in the world, and actively to teach all groups to respect each other. It is now more widely understood that Britain cannot afford – politically, socially or economically – to raise white monocultural young people, who regard racially and culturally different citizens of their own and other countries as inferior and alien. The education system has, for over 100 years, nurtured in young white people a jingoistic superiority based on ignorance and stereotyping, rather than a respect and understanding based on knowledge. In seeking to develop multicultural and non-racist education in white areas, schools are actively participating in a redefinition of 'what it means to live in British society' and what it means to 'be British'.

Central Government initiatives

The emergence of a broader view of multicultural education to include white pupils can be traced through a series of central government publications from 1977, although the rather optimistic theme that white pupils would be 'enriched' by the presence of minority pupils was articulated in a Ministry of Education publication as early as 1963. A Ministry pamphlet suggested then that 'our visitors from overseas' could 'give immediacy and meaning to our geography and history lessons, their contributions from the arts of their own countries can add interest and variety to many school occasions, their differing religions, customs, dress and food can provide most useful and immediate materials for the inculcation of at least some measure of international understanding' (Ministry of Education, 1963). HMI surveys in 1970 and 1971 continued the theme that multi-ethnic schools could become prototypes of a cohesive and tolerant multicultural society and that white pupils were being provided with unique opportunities for broadening their knowledge (DES, 1971).

In the event, the assimilationist pressures of the 1960s and 1970s meant that schools did not regard the presence and cultures of minority children as a resource, but rather as a problem, and many educational and curriculum opportunities were lost in both multi-ethnic and white schools. Evidence collected by the House of Commons Select Committee on Race Relations and Immigration during this period, ran counter to Department of Education optimism and indicated that white parents and pupils, far from welcoming and learning from ethnic minorities, were hostile and antagonistic to their presence. The white parent who demanded re-housing in Liverpool so that his children did not have to be 'educated with coons' (Select Committee, 1973, vol. 3, p. 557) was articulating a consistent, if unpleasant, populist white view that the presence and cultures of ethnic minorities stigmatized rather than enriched schools.

However, central government developed their view that education and, more specifically, the curriculum was to be a major influence in combating white populist views, in sustaining the idea of a multicultural British society and in offering pupils a more adequate understanding of the interdependence of nations. The 1977 Green Paper *Education in Schools – A Consultative Document*, produced under a Labour government, laid out very clearly government expectations of the role of the curriculum in a new kind of British society.

> Our society is a multi-cultural and multi-racial one and the curriculum should reflect a sympathetic understanding of the different cultures and races that now make up our society. We also live in a complex inter-dependent world and many of our problems in Britain require international solutions; the curriculum should therefore reflect our need to know about and understand other countries.
>
> (DES, 1977, p. 41)

This paper suggested that a major reason for the reluctance of educationalists to make appropriate curricular changes, was the influence of a colonial-imperial past which still fuelled beliefs in the superiority of all things British. The paper stated unequivocally that 'the curriculum appropriate to our imperial past cannot meet the requirements of modern Britain'. (p. 4). A conservative government, elected in 1979, continued to support a policy of providing a more appropriate and relevant education for pupils in all parts of Britain. A Minister of State for Education spoke at a Conference organized by the Commission for Racial Equality in 1980 on the importance of multicultural education in schools where there were no ethnic minority pupils, and of developing a curriculum which 'draws positive advantages from different cultures' (Young, 1980).

Curriculum documents produced by DES through the 1980s asserted the importance of the curriculum in helping all pupils to come to terms with a multicultural Britain and suggested that curriculum objectives in all subject areas would be related to this goal. The 1981 paper on *The School Curriculum* (DES, 1981a), which set the scene for the major curriculum reforms of the 1980s, reiterated the theme that 'our society has become multicultural' (p. 21), and amongst a list of the major purposes of learning set out in the paper, included two of direct relevance. Learning should specifically 'help pupils to develop personal moral values, respect for religious values, and tolerance of other races, religious and ways of life' and should 'help pupils understand the world in which they live and the interdependence of individual groups and nations'. While teaching tolerance and under-standing may be viewed by some practitioners as utopian, this curriculum paper also insisted that a major purpose of learning was to give pupils 'the ability to question and to argue rationally'. It is the ability to argue rationally that is a prerequisite to understanding why the British nation now includes non-white citizens, and why it makes little social, moral, political or economic sense to deny that they are equal citizens deserving of equal respect and opportunities. However, it is this ability which is often conspicuous by its absence in debates on race, culture and education.

The Committee of Enquiry into the education of ethnic minority children, set up in 1979, recognized that rational argument depended on prior information and knowledge, and considered that majority society pupils were often denied even basic knowledge about their minority group fellow citizens. In their 1981 interim report, this committee advised the government that 'accurate information must be made available on the historical and economic reasons for immigration to Britain, and on Britain's role in a interdependent world both past and present' (DES, 1981b).

The 1985 government white paper on *Better Schools* (DES, 1985b) continued to promote the view that the curriculum should be a major vehicle for bringing about an acceptance of social change. It acknowledged that British society had become more complex and diverse, that Britain's place in the world had changed, and that social, economic, and demographic changes had profoundly altered the circumstances in which schools work. *Better Schools* laid down that 'all pupils need to understand and acquire a positive attitude to the variety of ethnic groups within British society' (p. 61) and that this should be a major curriculum objective both in specified subject areas and in permeating the ethos of all schools. The document also noted that multicultural curriculum objectives were embodied in the national criteria laid down for the General Certificate of Secondary Education examinations, and in the criteria for initial teacher training (DES, 1984).

The final report of the Committee of Enquiry into the education of ethnic minority pupils (DES, 1985a) which, under the Chairmanship of Lord Swann from 1981, had turned itself into a committee enquiring into the education of all pupils in a multicultural society, was published in the same month as *Better Schools*. The Swann report stressed the relevance to schools and LEAs of changing the curriculum, producing policies, and generally ensuring that a more appropriate education would in future, be offered to all pupils.[1] However, the Committee was not optimistic that change would easily happen in white schools.

> It seems as though central government, having decided to shift the emphasis of multicultural education to embrace all schools, feels that by constant reiteration and exhortation to this effect, the message will somehow permeate all-white schools with no further effort or resources.
>
> (DES, 1985a, p. 228)

The research in white areas carried out for the committee certainly indicated that up to 1984 schools with few or no minority pupils had made little effort to revise their curriculum, or develop policies, and tended to dismiss multicultural education as 'not our concern', 'a very low priority', 'likely to be divisive or counter-productive'. White areas were, by and large, equating multicultural education with the presence of ethnic minority pupils; the concept of being part of a multicultural society had impinged little on the consciousness of schools with few or no ethnic minorities.

Having access to the Swann report before publication however, the government had decided that one response to this situation would be to offer resources via the Education Support Grant (ESG) programme, initiated by the 1984 Education (Grants and Awards) Act. This programme was designed to target central government resources on problems which needed national solutions (DES, 1987) and Educational Needs in a Multi-ethnic Society *was* considered one of 21 problems which needed a 'national solution'. From September 1985, 35 projects in this area were funded in 25 Local Education Authorities, the onus being placed on LEAs to write bids and promise support for such projects. By 1986 it had become apparent that some white LEAs were still reluctant to consider the issue as their concern and HMI held a conference in Buxton, Derbyshire, to persuade such authorities that reflecting the ethnic diversity of British society was of relevance to them. An Education Minister addressed this conference and noted that few people now disputed the Swann Committee conclusion that all children in all parts of the country should be prepared for life in an ethnically diverse Britain. He told Chief Education Officers of white counties that 'your task in county LEAs of providing an education appropriate for such a society may be more difficult in some ways than that of your colleagues from the cities, . . . you therefore face a particular challenge.' (Patten, 1986)

The challenge was presented as a series of questions: How in schools which are all-white or nearly all-white can you best reflect this ethnic diversity through the content of the curriculum? How can that curriculum be presented without bias or prejudice? How can the ethos in your schools promote understanding and respect for different ethnic groups? (Pattern, *op. cit.*). The Minister could fairly report that by 1986 a series of initiatives to encourage an appropriate education in white areas had been taken. These included:

☐ Setting out conditions for the approval of initial teacher training courses. From 1984 the Council for the Accreditation of Teacher Education required evidence that all students would receive training for a multicultural society before accrediting a course;

☐ An extension of the Grant-Related In-Service Training (GRIST). From September 1986 'teaching and the curriculum in a multi-ethnic society' was made a national INSET priority and short courses for senior staff in primary and secondary schools were developed on the understanding that senior staff are best placed to encourage innovation;

☐ Requiring the General Certificate of Secondary Education (GCSE) Examining Boards to have regard for cultural and linguistic diversity;

☐ Agreeing with the Schools Curriculum Development Committee that all its projects should continue to have regard for ethnic diversity;

☐ Raising the awareness of local education authorities to the importance of up-to-date and balanced information and teaching methods, much of this advice being offered by local advisors and HMI at regional and national level;

☐ Providing Education Support Grants (ESG) in predominantly white areas for curriculum and other development projects. By 1988 120 projects in all parts of Britain had been funded or promised funding, the majority in white areas.

With pressures emanating from the top downwards, from the Department of Education and Science, and 'bottom-up' from practitioners, a majority of local Education authorities had, by the 1980s produced, or were in the process of producing, policy statements on education for a multi-ethnic society, and were requiring action to be taken by schools. A Commission for Racial Equality survey in 1987 recorded that out of 115 LEAs in England, Scotland and Wales, 77 had some kind of policy produced or in production (CRE, 1987) and a survey by Robertson of 104 LEAs in 1988, produced replies from 64 (Robertson, 1988). A number of these however, were 'white' LEAs who replied that they had, as yet, no formal policy, and one Welsh authority replied on bilingually-headed notepaper that multicultural education was not relevant to the authority. Robertson also circulated 100 schools to attempt to assess the extent and nature of school multicultural policy developments and received replies and documentation from 34. It became clear that some action was taking place at both LEA and school level in white areas, but in the absence of more research the extent and nature of initiatives was still a matter for conjecture.

Educational policies and initiatives are both produced within and constrained by the current political climate. There have been, throughout the 1980s, signs of tension between the multicultural education policies supported by the Department of Education and Science and the majority of local authorities, and also between some government ministers, politicians, and interest groups. The right wing of the Conservative party has always been opposed to multicultural education and to the proposals of the Swann Committee. A Monday Club paper produced after the appearance of the Swann report, recorded opposition to the use of the education system to 'promote foreign tongues, customs and religions' (Pearce, 1985). Multicultural, anti-racist education has been successfully vilified, not without some help from the left, as a neo-Marxist political activity (Honeyford, 1988) and the politicization of multicultural education by both right- and left-wing politicians, activists and interest groups, has un- doubtedly alienated many practitioners (see Tomlinson, 1987).

The 1988 Education Reform Act did not take the development of educational policy and practice in a multi-ethnic society forward on a statutory level. There was no mention anywhere in the Act of multicultural, non-racist education or of education appropriate for a multi-ethnic society. The number of opposition amendments defeated or withdrawn, as the legislation passed through Parliament, gave some indication of the determination of the government that the Act should not be explicit on issues of race or ethnicity.

The most important attempt to incorporate a racial dimension was an amendment put foreword by Lord Pitt of Hampstead, one of Britain's first black Peers. This suggested that the first clause of the Act, which requires the national curriculum to prepare pupils 'for the opportunities, responsibilities and experiences of adult life' should continue, 'in a multicultural, multi-racial society'. However, this amendment was eventually withdrawn. Likewise a proposal in the House of Lords to incorporate into the Act a sentence from page 61 of *Better Schools* (DES, 1985b) that all pupils be educated to acquire positive attitudes to all ethnic groups, was defeated by government supporters. Opposition Peers, in conjunction with the legal section of the Commission for Racial Equality, also sought to amend the requirements on open admission and parental choice of schools, to prevent these policies leading to racial segregation by school. Although Ministers had already conceded that such segregation could result from the Act, this amendment also had to be withdrawn (see Commission for Racial Equality, 1988).

However, the National Curriculum Council, set up in August 1988 to oversee the introduction of the national curriculum, was instructed from the outset by the Secretary of State to take account of ethnic and cultural diversity and the need to promote equal opportunities; the members of the Council were broadly sympathetic to this require- ment.[2] There does appear to be scope within the national curriculum to develop curriculum initiatives to provide a more appropriate education for all in a multi-ethnic society.

Literature on education in white areas

A general literature on multicultural education in Britain was relatively limited until well into the 1970s, but over the past ten years there has been a considerable increase in the variety of literature which

claims to be multicultural and anti-racist. To date, there has been no synthesis and analysis of this literature as, for example, Sleeter and Grant have done for multicultural education in the USA (Sleeter and Grant, 1987). In Britain the expanding literature has been concerned mainly with issues and polemics related to the education of ethnic minority pupils – particularly issues of achievement and curriculum – and with explorations of inequality and racism. Literature on the education of white pupils in a multi-ethnic society was virtually absent until the 1980s, although in 1971 McNeal and Rogers did propose that their analysis of the educational needs of pupils in multiracial schools should include white English children and that they were simply describing a rational approach for all schools (McNeal and Rogers, 1971, p. 15). In 1972, Townsend and Brittan, carrying out a preliminary survey for a Schools Council project aimed at producing curriculum materials for a multiracial society, reviewed replies from 126 headteachers in schools in white areas, agreeing that the curriculum *should* aim to prepare all pupils for life in a multiracial society. The Heads were unsure, however, how to put this aim into practice (Townsend and Brittan, 1973). The turning point seems to have been 1984, when literature began to emerge relating multicultural education to the majority white society, and to the provision of an appropriate education for a modern world in which white British children must learn to collaborate with people from different national, cultural and racial backgrounds.

A short but pertinent analysis of the pervasive nature of 'white superiority' was provided by Davis, a London advisor, in 1984. He began his analysis from the premise that the normal education system is based on the view that only the knowledge, values and beliefs of certain groups of white people is considered worthy of transmission and that the 'white ethnocentric system' perpetuates a deeply held belief in the superiority of white people (Davis, 1984). The important questions, for Davis, are not related to cultural diversity, but to why educationists need to perpetuate an irrational belief in the superiority of white people. Through an examination of section 7 of the 1944 Education Act (which requires LEAs to ensure that 'efficient education . . . shall be available to meet the needs of the population of their area'), he concluded that an approach to schooling based on beliefs in white superiority would never qualify as 'efficient'. Davis worried that an increase in policy statements on multicultural education led to good intentions on paper and little else. He considered that a multicultural approach should be the responsibility of all educational administrators and practitioners so that 'normal' education became an education appropriate for an historically multicultural nation.

Reports published in 1984 on behalf of the Church of England and the Catholic Church indicated Church concern that education in white Britain ought to address the issues. *Schools and Multicultural Education* was published by the Board of Education of the General Synod of the Church of England in April 1984, and *Learning from Diversity – a challenge for Catholic Education*, by a working party on Catholic Education for a Multiracial, Multicultural society in July. Both reports stressed that the diversity of British society required a broader educational approach and should not be narrowly Anglo-Saxon. 'A British-and-World perspective might more adequately reflect the cultural diversity of modern Britain and be a more appropriate foundation from which to develop educational approaches' (Working party on Catholic Education, 1984, p. 15).

Both reports endorsed a multi-faith approach to religious education and to the study of religions other than Christianity, and both reports deplored personal racism and prejudice, and racism on a structural level. The Catholic report referred to racism as 'a sickness of white society which needs to be healed' (p. 44) and noted that 'prejudiced attitudes among the staff, pupils and parents of any schools are a reality which education has to come to terms with and which cannot be glossed over by the fact that there are no explicit or violent racial incidents in the school' (p. 18).

The Churches' commitment to a more appropriate education in all areas may not yet, however, have affected schools. O'Keefe (1986) in a study of how 103 Church of England schools saw their role in a multicultural, multiracial, multi-faith society, had to report that teachers did take the view that multicultural education was only relevant if ethnic minorities were present. 'The concept of multi-cultural education being of relevance to all children, including those attending all-white or all Christian schools, has failed to impinge in practice on the majority of schools in our study' (p. 148).

In 1984 Taylor, a teacher-trainer at Exeter University, and a pioneer of both literature on, and teacher-training in, white areas, produced a seminal article which was entitled 'Multicultural Education in a Monocultural Region' (Taylor, 1984). He pointed out that the majority of the British population does not live in inner cities nor in regular contact with non-white people, and that this fact seemed to provide educationists in white areas with an excuse for dismissing thoughts of changing the school curriculum to accommodate to changes in British society. He described some cautious innovations in the predominantly rural and agricultural south-west of England, and suggested that in white, conservative areas, teachers needed to adopt a 'low key' approach to issues of culture, race, and racism. This view has subsequently been echoed in later literature and in teacher practice in white areas. Taylor articulated a general view of resistance to multicultural education in white areas when he noted that

> in attempting to innovate against apathy, suspicion and rationalisation, teachers interested in giving pupils an awareness of the benefits of multiculturalism and a knowledge of its ubiquitous presence throughout the world, will not be seen as responding to parental and communal needs: instead they are likely to incur opposition to what will be viewed as irrelevant to pupils needs. (Taylor, 1984, p. 6)

Taylor has also written strongly against what he sees as an international tendency for conservative educationalists, both black and white, to equate multicultural education with token symbols and customs rather than with institutional racism and personal racial prejudice.

Taylor's view has been put forward by writers in other countries, notably Bullivant in Australia (1984, 1986) and Moodley in Canada (1986), as well as in the 'multi-cultural versus anti-racist' debate in Britain (Craft, 1986; Troyna, 1987). Taylor's (1986) view was that while the Swann report had encouraged teachers in white areas to question the concept of culture in their own locality, many were still alarmed by the prospect of facing issues of racism and prejudice. He articulated the view that predominantly white schools should make an explicit response to racial injustice and has worked to produce racism-awareness training materials for white areas (Taylor, 1987a).

Evidence had certainly been accumulating during the 1980s of racist opinions among children in white schools (DES, 1985a, p. 234; Mould, 1986; Supple, 1986) and of resistance to some teaching strategies to reduce or counter racist views (Cosway and Rodney, 1987), and since 1987 there has certainly been more widespread discussion in the literature about pedagogy and strategies for curriculum change.

In the 1970s there was a belief that debates on a multicultural curriculum for multiracial schools was dominated by academics and policy-makers (Jeffcoate, 1979). The literature on all-white schools in the 1980s suggests that it is practitioners rather than academics and administrators who are concerned to bring about change in the curriculum, and are writing about their efforts. Practitioners are 'talking to each other' in an informed and sophisticated manner through journal articles and conferences, and the contributions from ethnic minority teachers, teacher-trainers and advisors are ensuring that debates on education in white areas remain in touch with the actual experiences of those considered to be racially or ethnically different. Teacher-trainers, from the mid 1980s, began to focus more on the appropriate education of all teachers for a multi-ethnic society. How to plan effective in-service courses for teachers in white areas was the focus of a School Curriculum Development project in 1982/3 (Carter, 1985). This project explored curriculum and organizational developments through which teachers in three mainly white areas of the country could develop skills and confidence in making changes. Exchanges and twinning with schools in multi-ethnic areas was considered to be one successful strategy for teachers and pupils in white areas (p. 15).

The National Anti-Racist Movement in Education (NAME) held its annual conference for teachers in Chichester, Sussex, in 1987 on the theme of 'anti-racist education in white areas', and the conference proceedings were then published (NAME, 1987). This conference indicated that the 'multi-cultural versus anti-racist' debate, which had dominated much of the race and education literature in the 1980s, had ceased to be an issue polarizing practitioners. The two concepts were usually joined in one phrase and were not regarded as mutually exclusive. The conference proceedings demonstrated that there were, to date, no theoretical models of an appropriate education for all in white areas which could be drawn upon by practitioners, but it was likely that any such models would develop from practical activity.

Troyna, who worked in schools and colleges in north-east England between 1986 and 1988, has suggested that issues of racial inequality and injustice can 'only be broached seriously and effectively through more broadly conceived programmes of political education' (Troyna, 1988, p. 6), a position that is reminiscent of the work of the Brazilian educator Paulo Freire in the 1970s (Freire, 1971). Troyna has directed attention to the importance of pedagogy and strategies for curriculum change in white areas, and suggested that authoritarian and didactic teaching is not congruent with discussions of oppression and injustice. Pedagogic strategies are certainly an issue apparent in the ESG projects described later in this book.

The 1987 NAME Conference organizer was Chris Gaine, who has produced the first full-length book on education in white areas. In *No Problem Here* (Gaine, 1987) Gaine aptly reiterates a continuing refrain from teachers in areas with few or no ethnic minorities who claim that issues of race and cultural diversity do not concern them. Gaine offered a good deal of practical advice to teachers in white areas. His account of setting up and teaching a social studies course in which race was a major element provided an honest and instructive example of the problems and pitfalls inherent in both the subject matter and teaching strategies. It was particularly depressing to read that his white pupils were not interested in cultural attributes:

They do not listen to the distinction between Sikhs, Muslims, Gujeratis and Bengalis, West Indians and Indians, because they are not interested, they do not want to know because the important thing to them is that these people are not white, and the students believe they are responsible for all the unemployment and bad housing.

(Gaine, 1987, p. 86)

In the 1980s the journal *Multi-Cultural Teaching* provided an important venue for practitioners in white areas to describe examples of changed practice in their schools, and to criticize their own strategies and pedagogy. The Summer 1986 issue focused on the north-east of England as 'this region of Britain is a fertile breeding ground for crude racist activity and propaganda' (Editorial, *Multi-Cultural Teaching*, vol. 4, no. 3, 1986). However, all five local education authorities in the north-east region have produced policy statements for education for a multiracial society, and Newcastle upon Tyne has a policy for all city council departments. Five articles in the Spring 1987 issue of *Multi-Cultural Teaching* addressed issues of education in white areas, beginning with a moving memoir by Trudi Levi, a victim of Nazi racism in the 1940s (Levi, 1987). Massey described the way in which a working party in his Hampshire school used the Swann recommendations to make changes which permeated the whole school (Massey, 1987), and the headteacher of a Kent primary school offered positive suggestions for adding a multicultural dimension to the primary school curriculum in white areas. He noted that 'it is useless to pretend that the majority white population of Britain does not have fears about sharing this island with other ethnic groups' and offered suggestions to allay predictable fears (Cartwright, 1987, p. 11). Articles in the journal have consistently articulated the theme that multicultural and anti-racist education is a concern for all schools. Hopkin (1987) described the development of a multicultural anti-racist policy in a white working-class school, where despite racist attacks and behaviour exhibited by some of the local community, teachers were initially reluctant to involve themselves in developments, and Cosway (1988) published an 'institutional Racism' checklist for both multi-ethnic and all-white schools.

Research studies of multicultural innovation and developments in white schools is still minimal, much of the literature being on the descriptive level, offering guidance to others. *Perspectives 35* from the University of Exeter, offered a series of articles written by teachers working in the south-west of England but who had previously worked in Britain's inner cities. The teachers had participated in a day conference at which a standing conference on Multicultural Education in the South-West was set up (Taylor, 1987b). A further source of information on white areas are small-scale studies undertaken by teachers on advanced study courses. Anne Taylor (1988) studied two Cumbrian schools that were attempting to incorporate multicultural perspectives in the curriculum. She noted that in both these schools 'few teachers were addressing the theoretical principles of multi-cultural education with clarity, and many were unsure about its relevance and possibility for pedagogic application. Most of the teachers, however, did acknowledge that multicultural education was relevant and particularly referred to racism in the county, and the need to widen the experiences of the children' (A. Taylor, 1988, p. 6).

Roberts (1987), writing in the journal of the National Union of Teachers, criticized the attitude of the Department of Education and Science to work in white schools during the passing of the 1988 Act through Parliament. Roberts's Hampshire school, filmed for BBC TV schools programme on racism (BBC TV, 1987) developed a policy based on the Swann Committee recommendations and the Hampshire LEA's response to Swann. He deplored the lack of consultation over multicultural issues in the National Curriculum, and the lack of leadership offered by senior Ministers.

> People at the top should be publicly stating that racism is evil and . . . those schools trying their best, in sensitive ways, to change racism should be commended. On the other hand, teachers must cease to give the impression that they are acting in a maverick way – they must consult at every level in a democratic way on any proposal for curriculum change in schools (p. 49).

Richardson, an education advisor, has been more overtly critical of the 1988 Education Act and what he sees as a retreat from racial equality policies by both central and local authorities (Richardson, 1988). He took the view that a major effect of the Act will be to shift influence away from teachers and advisors, who are the people most concerned with innovation in white schools.

Teachers' unions have so far been relatively muted in their support for a more appropriate multicultural curriculum in white schools. The most comprehensive and forward-looking statement has been pro-duced by the Assistant Masters and Mistresses Association (AMMA, 1987). This statement concedes that understanding the nature and purpose of a multicultural curriculum is much more widespread now, but notes that 'Regrettably, some people still feel that a multicultural approach is irrelevant to their monocultural school . . . and some still reject the multicultural curriculum as irrelevant to the target of eradicating racism' (p. 8).

As far as the most recent developments in schools in white areas are concerned, there is a small but growing literature produced by

Education Support Grant project workers. Such literature will eventually provide a comprehensive picture of developments and practices in white areas in the 1980s and 1990s (see chapter five).

Some conclusions to be drawn from the 'white' schools literature so far indicate:

☐ that there is still a range of negative views about the implementation of a more appropriate education for a multi-ethnic society. These views range from outright hostility and suspicion, through apathy, indifference and a denial that the issues do affect the school and the area;

☐ that strategies for curriculum change and implementation of multicultural initiatives in white areas, by the small but growing number of committed practitioners must be 'low-key' and include democratic consultation with colleagues and the community;

☐ that antagonistic debates over multicultural versus anti-racist adduction have little relevance for white areas, where cultural and global education, and education against racism are seen as necessary, but practitioners should still be wary of token curriculum change only concerned with cultural symbols;

☐ that there are as yet no developed theoretical models of an appropriate education for white areas, although one possible model is that of a broad political education which takes account of class, gender and racial inequalities;

☐ that the literature is predominantly emanating upwards from practitioners rather than being the production of academics or policy-makers;

☐ that there is considerable uncertainty about how the requirements of the 1988 Education Act and in particular, the national curriculum, will affect multicultural and non-racist developments in the 1990s

Plan of the Book

The direction of central government initiatives, local education authority and school responses, indicates that there has been, since 1985, a positive reaction to the Swann Committee's view that to educate all pupils appropriately for a multi-ethnic society, change will be required, particularly in all-white areas. Yet there is also widespread resistance to this view, and the educational climate post-1988 may encourage inertia or reverses, rather than progress. This book addresses itself to two questions. First, why is there such strong resistance to the idea that a change in education is necessary for a multi-ethnic Britain and an interdependent world? And second, what sort of initiatives and developments are in progress in schools in white areas? The focus here is on the central government initiative providing Education Support Grants for multicultural projects in these areas.

Chapter one examines the growing uncertainty about what constitutes 'being British' in a 'British nation' with a 'British cultural heritage'. There is considerable resistance to discarding ideas, beliefs, and values associated with a period of imperial dominance. The chapter explores the concept of national identity, political resistance to accepting minorities as part of the nation and a developing educational nationalism. Chapter two examines evidence of inappropriate beliefs and attitudes among teachers, pupils and parents towards racial and cultural minorities in Britain. The extent of white pupil hostility to, and stereotyping of, minorities, is slowly being documented, but schools are still not geared to tackling the extent of ignorance and prejudice. Chapter three suggests that one reason for the strong resistance to change in education is the legacy of the imperial curriculum of the late Victorian and Edwardian period. The development of compulsory schooling, the expansion of textbook publishing and juvenile literature coincided with a period of high imperialism, when the militaristic imperial values of public schools filtered down to state schooling.

Chapter four reviews opposition to the kind of curriculum change envisaged by the Swann committee, describes some of the literature produced by subject specialists who have suggested changes in their subject areas and considers the moves towards incorporating a multicultural dimension in the national curriculum. Chapter five describes the ESG programme funded by the DES from 1985 in 'Education for a Multi-Ethnic Society' and introduces the research study on 24 projects carried out in 1987–8. Chapters six and seven provide a descriptive analysis of the projects, ranging from Cumbria and Tyneside in the North of England, to Kent and Wiltshire in the South. The curriculum innovation and in-service work undertaken by practitioners in white areas are positive moves forward in the task of providing a more appropriate education. Chapter eight considers the magnitude of the task of changing education for a multi-ethnic society and whether a developing 'educational nationalism' will actually reverse positive changes.

Notes

1   *Selected Recommendations of the Swann Report* (DES, 1985a, p. 364).

☐ All Local Education authorities should declare their commitment to the principles of Education for All, to the development of a pluralist approach to the curriculum and to countering the influence of racism.

☐ Every LEA should have at least one advisor and perhaps a Senior Officer with responsibility to promote the policies we have put forward, to act as a catalyst to encourage teachers and other advisors to adopt a pluralist perspective in their work.

☐ All LEAs should expect their schools to produce clear policy statements on 'Education For All' and monitor this practical implementation.

☐ All schools, whether multi-racial or all-white, should review their work in the same light of the principles we have put forward.

☐ All schools should adopt clear policies to combat racism.

2 In particular, one member of the National Curriculum Council was a headteacher of a school with pupils of predominantly Bangladeshi origin, and another was a black lecturer and broadcaster (Mrs Daphne Gould and Ms Beverley Anderson.)

1 The British national identity

> It is important for people living today to understand how they came to be what they are, to appreciate the forces and events that have shaped the institutions which guide and govern us, and generally to recognise how our rich and complex past has shaped what we think of as our national identity.
> (Secretary of State for Education, K. Baker, 1988, p. xxi)

In the modern world, claims to nationhood, the recognition of national identities, and the relationship between national majorities and ethnic minorities living in the same territory are all matters for intense international debate. The issues are not academic. People are prepared to die for the recognition of their national or their ethnic identity, and ethnic conflicts within nations are a world-wide phenomenon (Smith, 1986).

As the post-war migration into Britain of groups variously perceived by the white majority to be racially, ethnically or culturally different[1] has now ended, and the incorporation of these groups as permanent settlers and citizens has begun, questions about what it means to be part of a British nation, and to share a national identity and a cultural heritage, have begun to be raised in a variety of forms. In the educational literature the issue of national identity has to some extent been submerged by assertions that Britain *is* or *ought* to be recognized as a multiracial, multi-ethnic, multicultural, or culturally plural society, and by debate over the meaning of these concepts and their relevance (Bolton, 1979; Troyna, 1982; Tomlinson, 1983; DES, 1985a; Craft, 1984, 1986). Much of this literature offered a description and critique of educational policies and adaptation to ethnic diversity from the 1950s, and discussed the extent of movement from assimilationist views of minority cultures to greater acknowledgement and recognition of these cultures in the 1980s. While this literature also acknowledged and discussed the extent of racism in British society and in education, a more radical literature has insisted that the fundamental response to ethnic minorities in education has been conditioned by racism and by a denial of resources, power and equal opportunities (Mullard, 1982, 1984; ILEA, 1983; Brandt, 1986).

Although most of the educational writers have acknowledged, implicitly or explicitly, that the majority of consumers of education in Britain do not appear to believe that they live in a multi-ethnic or multicultural society and have noted a strong populist resistance to the acceptance of non-white groups as equal citizens in the British nation, the reasons for this resistance have not so far been analysed in any great detail. Frequent polemical and emotive assertions that racism is *the* problem have proved unhelpful, without further analysis and elaboration of why beliefs in white superiority are so pervasive and so enduring. On the other hand, literature which suggests that racism is simply a figment of a looney-left imagination, or a Marxist-inspired conspiracy, is equally unhelpful.

What has to be acknowledged, though, is that while liberal and socialist writers and educationalists have engaged in conceptual debates about the nature of a multicultural society, definitions of multicultural education and the need for anti-racist education, the white majority population has been more interested in and influenced by those who deny the reality and permanence of a multicultural British society, and resists the suggestion that education has a role to play in educating all pupils more appropriately for such a society.

Increasingly popular now are the arguments of those who start from the premise that there is an unproblematic British national identity, that it is underpinned by an unproblematic British heritage and British culture, and that the claims of non-white citizens to be included within the boundaries of this national identity are suspect. These views have proved more acceptable to the white majority population than any debates prefaced by 'multi' or 'anti'.

Because the supporters of a more appropriate education for multi-ethnic Britain have ignored the question of national identity, the parameters of the debate have been set by politicians, the media and some academics and educationalists who have been described as part of the 'new right' (Palmer, 1985; Mishan, 1988), although some of their ideas have a distinctly 'old' flavour. They start from the premise that it was an unfortunate mistake to have allowed the settlement of Asian and Afro-Caribbean people who can never become part of the British nation. Thus:

> The omnipresence in his native land today of peoples of Afro-Asian origin with whom the white Briton does not share the pride of a common heritage or culture, and with whom he cannot, in the nature of things, share that atavistic sense of kith and kin, acts over time to confuse his sense of national wholeness and to weaken his sense of national identity.
>
> (Mishan, 1988, p. 18)

This chapter examines ambivalent ministerial views of the national identity, the crisis of national identity, political resistance to Britain as a multi-ethnic society, and a developing nationalism in education. The chapter briefly makes out an economic case for multicultural global education rather than educational nationalism.

Ministerial views

The Swann report (DES, 1985a) took as its ideological starting point the view that Britain has long been a pluralist society in which regional variations and sub-cultural groupings are accepted as part of a British way of life. But the committee recognized that calling for an extension of this pluralism to embrace non-white minority cultures was likely to be interpreted by some as seeking to undermine 'an ill-defined and nebulous concept of true Britishness'. It is this concept which national leaders, including education ministers, find it difficult to define or relinquish when the question is raised of the inclusion of ethnic-minorities and aspects of their culture in a British way of life. Despite an official policy which asserts that Britain is a multi-ethnic society with an education system which must adapt to this, Ministers of Education in the 1980s have typified a general ambivalence over the acceptance of the cultures, histories and languages of ethnic minorities as part of British life, and have avoided exploration of what this means in terms of a changed national identity. They have continued to present 'being British' with British values and a national heritage as an unproblematic static concept, rather than a concept which is both dynamic and in need of critical examination.

This is, in part, a reflection of the educational debate on unity versus diversity within nation-states that have experienced immigration of ethnic minorities since the Second World War. This debate centres on the question as to how far education systems can tolerate diversity of values without putting at risk the social cohesion supposedly produced by a curriculum reflecting a common culture and shared cultural values (see Craft, 1984; Banks and Lynch, 1986). But it is also a reflection of a general unwillingness to submit the majority culture, with its assumptions of shared values and a common heritage, to much-needed scrutiny. The ambivalence towards minority cultures was expressed in 1986 by a Minister of State for Education, who asserted at a conference of HMI,

> I believe that in areas where there are few or no members of ethnic minority groups, there is a genuine and not dishonourable fear that British values and traditions – the very stuff of school education – are likely to be put at risk if too much allowance is made for the cultural backgrounds and attitudes of ethnic minorities.

(Patten, 1986)

By focusing on the minority cultures and values as problematic, attention is directed from the need to question and examine the nature of British values and traditions, and reassess whether these values are appropriate in late twentieth-century society. If British values are indeed the 'very stuff of school education' then it is right that they should be subject to scrutiny.

A similar ambivalence was reflected in the final statement of Sir Keith Joseph, Secretary of State for Education between 1981 and 1985, when he left office in May 1985. He reaffirmed his belief that Britain was now an ethnically mixed society, that minority cultures should be acknowledged in schools and that racial prejudice must be eliminated, but he also reiterated an unproblematic and mythologized view of British values and cultural traditions. His statement referred to a 'tradition of tolerance' being one of Britain's most 'precious virtues', and of an 'accumulated richness' of the national culture owing much to 'contacts with other people'. 'British history and cultural traditions are, or will become, at least part of a common heritage of all who live in this country. . . . Schools should be responsible for trying to transmit British culture, enriched as it has been by so many traditions' (Joseph, 1986).

The problem with assertions of positive values of tolerance and enrichment is that a study of any history of British imperial contacts with other people, even one sympathetic to the development of the British Empire (for example Lloyd, 1984), demonstrates that these contacts mainly took the form of military conquests, appropriation of land and wealth, subjugation of peoples, slavery, forced labour, forced migration, oppression and denial of human rights. Similarly, studies of the British response to the immigration of former imperial subjects has from the 1950s demonstrated systematic discrimination, denial of rights and a conspicious lack of a tradition of tolerance (Smith, 1977; Rex and Tomlinson, 1979; Dummett, 1983).

A major problem in presenting the history and heritage of any group is that it is – and perhaps must be – composed of mythological elements. People need to create an idealized view of their heritage, and stress the most positive characteristics of their supposed national identity. In Britain, a country which a century ago ruled a quarter of the world's territory, there appears to be a particular need for beliefs in a heritage of tolerance, fair play, and rule of law, even though actual historical behaviour deviated from these qualities. Inglis (1985) has pointed out that both curriculum theorists and exponents of multi-cultural education have avoided examining popular notions of British values and heritage as reflected in the school curriculum because close scrutiny of 'the stories we tell ourselves' about our history and heritage would be too uncomfortable. Myth and reality are too far apart. Nevertheless the present Secretary of State for Education has also presented a somewhat romanticized view of English history in a volume of selected verse published in 1988. He claimed that the verses offered a 'true sense of the narrative flow of our history' which not only document decisive events in history, but also demonstrate the 'dogged cheerfulness of ordinary people' (Baker, 1988, Introduction). The verses actually document conflict, battles, civil war, 'foreign' war and death, from Cowper on 'Boadicea' in AD 68 to Harrison on 'VJ Day' in 1945 and include one poem on slavery and several celebrating the acquisition of Empire and lamenting its loss. The qualities of ordinary people illustrated by the verses tend towards despair, anger and malice rather than tolerance and cheerfulness. Baker did eschew the verse of Scotland, Ireland and Wales except when 'their history becomes entwined' with English history, usually by battles and conquest. Nationalist views within these countries to the present day do assert that there territories have been 'internally colonised' by the English (Hechter, 1975), with their cultural and linguistic dominance and the attempted suppression of political and cultural nationalism that accompanies colonialism. In an interview after the publication of his book Mr Baker told an interviewer that 'I am an English patriot, I hope there is something of the nature of England in the book' (Faulks, 1988).

National identity

Those whose national identities have seldom been questioned and have never known the subjugation of their territory or culture, are able to claim that they have a unique and recognizable identity, usually based on a common ancestry and a shared history, and often defined by the exclusion of 'others' who have been conquered or colonized. Most English primary school children who have 'done the Romans' would recognize that Roman citizens made this claim 2000 years ago, and for much of the twentieth century the English are perhaps the people most likely to have made a similar claim. But, as Anthony Smith (1986) and other writers on the origins of nations have pointed out, the seemingly self-evident nature of a national identity is usually made up of a mixture of objective fact and subjective factors. The objective 'facts' about the nation are those such as demographic statistics, size of territory, kings and queens, dates of battles, while subjective factors, include collective values, beliefs, memories, shared symbols and myths. It is the values and the myths that are usually recorded in the art, literature, science and communication of the nation, and they shape each generation's view of what constitutes a national identity and a cultural heritage (Smith, 1986, p. 3). In the course of history, objective fact and myth easily become confused and what appears to be a shared history can be simply a collection of shared myths.

Those claiming a shared national identity will also subscribe to the doctrine of nationalism, which is concerned with the organized politics of a nation by which groups with power decide who will be included and who will be excluded from belonging to the nation. The German national socialism of the 1930s for example, recognized only those defined as Aryan as belonging to a German nation, and white South Africa similarly excludes black groups from participation in the nation. Goulbourne (1989) has pointed out that nationalism 'seeks to establish lines of communication between those who ostensibly belong to the fold, and at the same time establish clear boundaries for those who do not belong' (p. 6). National identity is threatened when minorities enter a society and begin to assert both a separate cultural position *and* a desire to be included in the nation.

One response of national majorities to this situation is to appeal to patriotism, a supposed fervent affiliation to a territory, which will exclude minority and immigrant groups. Goulbourne has noted that 'one of the great and renewable strengths of nationalism, is its ability to press-gang patriotism into active service' (p. 28). The literature of extreme right groups in Britain routinely uses appeals to a patriotic nationalism to exclude racial and ethnic minorities from the idea of a British nation.

Another common response of national majorities to the presence of minorities is to take up what Dench (1986) has described as a hypocritical position. The majority will demand that the minority 'assimilate' and adhere to the majority values, but at the same time treat the minorities differently and unequally. This has been the situation in Britain for the past 30 years, with many politicians and educators calling for the assimilation of minorities while ignoring the barriers of discrimination and denial of citizenship rights placed in their path. A question posed by both Dench and Goulbourne is whether ethnic minorities in liberal societies will ever successfully change their relationship with the national majority, by surmounting social barriers and injustice. This would mean pressuring the majority to abandon its hypocrisy and live up to the democratic and liberal principles it preaches.

A crucial question in Britain is whether people of 'non-white' ethnic background, particularly those of African, Caribbean and Asian origin will ever come to be regarded by the white population as equal citizens and whether they will be offered a genuine choice of cultural affiliation. The view of most black British scholars at the moment, is that a 'Black British' or 'Asian British' identity is not yet part of an acceptable image of post-imperial Britain (Gilroy, 1987; Hall, 1988; Goulbourne, 1989). There is a cultural and political resistance by the white majority to the conjunction of being 'black', or 'Asian', *and* British.

Empire and a crisis of identity

It is undoubtedly the case that the idea of a British national identity, and the exclusion of those considered to be racially unacceptable and culturally different, cannot be understood without some knowledge of the history of the British Empire, colonial expansion and imperial ideologies. The period 1870 –1920 is generally taken by historians to be the high point of Empire and imperialism, and was also (as chapter three documents) a period in which mass state schooling in England was developing. The consequences of the rule over large numbers of non-white people led to a variety of rationalizations for economic and political exploitation. Victorian thinking on race represented a complex collection of pseudo-scientific theories and economic and other interests, which created a set of stereotypes about non-white people, often portraying them as 'savage and bestial figures who needed to be controlled at all costs, and also as helpless beings in need of missionary care and protection' (Rich, 1986, p. 12). The liberal evangelical movement which had achieved the abolition of slavery in British colonies in the 1830s gradually gave way to a more powerful racial hostility based on economic exploitation. For example, Carlyle, a Victorian intellectual undoubtedly part of a British 'cultural heritage', contributed to the stereotype of a lazy and indolent black who should be forced to labour to 'bring out the products of the West Indian Islands for the benefit of all mankind' (Carlyle, 1849). In fact, the labourers on West Indian plantations particularly enriched white planters, several of whom returned to Britain to be incorporated into the British aristocracy, and also enriched the ports of Liverpool, London and Bristol, rather than either themselves or mankind.

The incorporation of Darwin's ideas of biological hierarchies into Victorian debates about the origin of races led to the doctrine of Social Darwinism and to claims of a genetic white British superiority over non-white races. Lloyd (1984) has noted that by the 1860s British opinion was moving to a simple regard for 'the empire's black and brown subjects as natural inferiors' (p. 180). The Victorian idea of a superior Anglo-Saxon race inhabiting Britain, developed at a time when the expansion of colonial settlement, particularly in Africa, was taking place. After a debate as to how far a Celtic influence should be included as part of a British national identity (Arnold, 1905) the

Anglo-Saxon 'race' was, by the turn of the century, popularly presented as the world's superior group: biologically, economically, politically, linguistically and culturally superior to colonized races and non-Anglo-Saxon nations. The idea of a 'blood brotherhood' of white nations was also propagated at this time (Murray, 1905) – an idea which has persisted into the twentieth century. Defence of white settlers in Zimbabwe during the war of independence in the 1970s was based on the populist idea of 'our kith and kin' being under attack. The strength of Victorian beliefs in white racial superiority has persisted through the ending of colonialism and imperial dominance, and the arrival of former colonial people into Britain, and has strongly influenced the perception of who belongs to the nation and who does not.

Beliefs in biological superiority were accompanied by ideas of cultural superiority over non-white imperial subjects. The strength of Victorian beliefs in a superior British culture can be exemplified by the views of Lord MacCauley on Indian culture. Speaking in a House of Commons debate in 1833, he noted that the British Empire illustrated the 'triumph of reason over barbarianism . . . the Empire is the imperishable Empire of our arts, morals, literature, and law.' The following year, presiding over the General Committee of Public Instruction in India, MacCauley recorded his view that he had not found an orientalist who 'could deny that a single shelf of a good European library was worth the whole native literature of India and Arabia' (quoted in Moorhouse, 1983, p. 77). It was MacCauley's influence that ensured that education in India from 1835 was based on Western science and literature, with English as the language of instruction.

The predominance of English as the language of Empire has had global repercussions in the twentieth century and there is no doubt that one legacy of Empire is that English is now a global common language. Since the sharing of a common language is the most common claim to nationhood, the use of English as a global language encourages the idea of a superiority of the 'English nation'. In addition minorities have been, and are, judged by their capacity to speak English as a condition of entry to nationhood. Minority languages, particularly the Asian languages derided by MacCauley, have been particularly considered to be of inferior status.

In the later twentieth century, notions of biological, cultural and linguistic superiority can only be sustained by a very selective perception of other nations and world events. But it does appear that the white majority in Britain is selectively holding on to remnants of Victorian beliefs in order to sustain a narrow, parochial and often intolerant view of 'who belongs' within the boundaries of a national identity.

One view emerging from those who have considered the national identity from the point of view of the 'colonized', is that as Britain completes a transition from imperial status and ruler of colonies to national status with a dwindling influence on world affairs, there is something of a crisis of national identity. Salman Rushdie, that perceptive chronicler of the painful creation of the nations of India and Pakistan, and the uneasy cultural relationships of Britain with former colonial territories, wrote in 1982: 'I believe Britain is undergoing a critical phase of its post-colonial period and this crisis is not simply economic or political. It is a crisis of the whole culture, of the society's whole sense of itself.' (Rushdie, 1982).

Rushdie and others (Hall, 1988) take the view that the British are, in the post-imperial period, attempting to reconstitute an image of themselves by defining who is *not* British, and those defined as non-white or ex-colonial are automatically excluded from the national identity. It certainly seems to be the case that by continuing to construct stereotyped images of inferior cultures and peoples, the white British are attempting to sustain an identity which cannot really be acceptable in an interdependent world, although Hall (1988) has suggested that it is only by doing this that the British 'know who they are'. Even in the 1980s the James Bond stories and films recreate a cultural fantasy in which 'orientals, wops, wogs and foreigners' (Hall, op. cit.) are stereotyped 'baddy's' to be set off against the 'goody' British. Fleming, the creator of James Bond, held racial views on the superiority of white over black and wrote that the black races were more timid, fearful and superstitious than white (Fleming, 1952, 1954).

The strength of ethnocentric cultural beliefs in the superiority of the 'white British' is partly sustained by film and fiction, but is also sustained in parts of the school curriculum. Remnants of the imperial curriculum and Victorian beliefs in racial and cultural superiority still permeate the modern curriculum, and sustain a cultural resistance to the idea that groups perceived as racially and culturally different and inferior can ever be part of the British nation (see chapter three).

Political resistance

There has been political resistance from both the left and the right to the idea that former imperial subjects and their children should be accepted as part of the British nation, and despite the election of four black MPs to Parliament in 1987, many politicians still do on occasions present immigrants and minorities as being a threat to the nation, rather than part of it. The Victorian conjunction between race and nation is still apparent in the presentation of the British nation as biographically and culturally exclusive and monocultural. Phrases such as 'This Island Race' and 'this bulldog breed' vividly convey the ideal of the nation as belonging to white people (Gilroy, 1987) and right-wing nationalist parties use the bulldog and the union jack as symbols of this exclusiveness. The concept of national belonging not only at times excludes non-whites but also uses militaristic and patriotic metaphors of war and invasion to describe immigrant minorities:

> The enemy within, the unarmed invasion, alien encampments, alien territory, new commonwealth occupations, have all been used to describe the black presence in this way.
>
> (Gilroy, *op. cit.*, p. 45)

The post-war Conservative position centred round the belief that all British citizens, of whatever colour, had equal rights before the law, although during the 1950s this was contested and Winston Churchill considered the possibility of using a 'keep Britain white' slogan in the 1955 General Election. In the 1960s Enoch Powell began what Rich (1986) has described as a populist quest against the Commonwealth and the search for a new English identity. His anti-immigration speech in April 1968 aroused extreme racist reactions. He received nearly 65,000 letters of support, 4000 white dockers went on strike in his support and marched to Westminster proclaiming 'Back Britain, not black Britain', and the Conservative MP for Stratford-upon-Avon declared that 'The British do not want a multiracial society any more than they want their grammar schools destroyed, their village schools closed or their telephone boxes painted yellow.' (*Independent*, 18.4.88, p. 5). Such was Powell's support that he could also attack the Queen for her attachment to the Commonwealth and support for her minority subjects; a headline in the *Sun* in 1984 proclaimed 'Enoch raps Queen – she must speak up more for whites' (*Sun*, 21.1.84.).

A long-term result of Powell's views has been a heightening of race consciousness in Britain and the reiteration of the idea that non-whites could somehow be 'repatriated'. In April 1988 an article entitled 'Enoch Powell – Midwife to the Spirit of a Nation' extolled his influence (Gimson, 1988), and he has not abandoned his view that the actual presence of non-white minorities constitutes a 'menacing' threat that will inevitably lead to civil discord (Powell in Lewis, 1988, Introduction).

The present Prime Minister has also presented the idea of the British nation as a superior, imperial power, resistant to alien cultures, and the 1982 Falklands War provided an opportunity to assert a patriotic imperialism which derided 'foreigners' (Thatcher, 1982).[2] During this war a *Sunday Telegraph* article asserted that:

> if the Falkland Islanders were British citizens with black or brown skins, spoke with strange accents or worshipped strange Gods, it is doubtful whether the Royal Navy or Marines would be fighting for their liberation.
>
> (Worsthorne, 23.5.82)

In the late 1980s, as European nations move closer together, the Prime Minister has suggested that a British national identity would be threatened by closer links with Europe, and has referred to more problems of 'illegal immigrants' if European frontier controls were abolished (Thatcher, 1988). There is however, no single Conservative position on the place of minorities within the nation. There are a variety of groups with views on minorities and multicultural education ranging from the liberal-conservative Bow Group (Gibson and Sadeque, 1988) to more extreme right-wing groups such as the Monday Club and Tory Action (see Gordon and Klug, 1986) who are opposed to any educational change for a multi-ethnic society and support repatriation. There are also academic groups, for example the Conservative Philosophy group, the Salisbury group and the Hillgate group, who oppose multiculturalism and support the educational nationalism described in the following section.

However, other Conservatives have voiced concern over ambivalent or hostile views of minorities held by some influential politicians. Sir David Lane, a former MP and first Chairman of the Commission for Racial Equality, has written that:

> It is lamentable that in eight years as Prime Minister Mrs Thatcher has not made a single speech denouncing racialism and discrimination and encouraging the work of justice and harmony.
>
> (Lane, 1987)

Unfortunately, though, electoral success still seems to be enhanced by the presentation of alien cultures swamping British values, of the presentation of all those opposing racism as 'looney-left agitators' (Layton-Henry, 1986) and of inner-cities as 'criminal sanctuaries controlled by young blacks' who pose a threat to law and order (*Times*, 19.11.85).

Socialist and left-wing groups have however often excluded ethnic minorities and their cultures, despite ideologies of the 'brotherhood of man' and universal human rights. The Labour politician Roy Hattersley spoke in 1966 of the need to 'make provision to teach these [immigrant] children basic British customs, British habits and if one likes, basic British prejudices' and the Labour Cabinet of Harold Wilson had accepted by 1965 that sympathy for 'immigrants' was a vote-loser (Crossman, 1979). A Labour Home secretary introduced an Immigration Control Act in 1968 and in the 1980s many trade unions, including the National Union of Teachers, have rejected demands for black sections. The socialist writer Raymond Williams analysed English working class resentment of 'unfamiliar neighbours' (Williams, 1983) and the Labour MP David Blunkett has focused on 'the crisis of cultural identity for us, the white British, half-Christian majority' (Blunkett, 1988). However, some left-inclined academics and practitioners have taken up positions which have provided an easy target for right-wing attacks, and have damaged a liberal quest for appropriate educational change. Right-wing attacks have been able to lump together all multiculturalists as potential left-wing subversives (see Palmer, 1986a).

Liberal individualism has, in the twentieth century, provided a basis for social reform and the acquisition of social and welfare rights. Roy Jenkins's 1966 speech extolling 'equal opportunity and cultural diversity in an atmosphere of mutual tolerance' came to embody a national goal for a liberal democracy. However, liberal social, community, and educational workers, attempting to create one nation out of a predominantly antagonistic white majority and increasingly vocal non-white minorities, have come under attack from all sides, being derided as 'do-gooders' or as part of a 'race relations industry'. The Owenite Social Democratic Party may be moving away from support for a democratic pluralism to an educational nationalism. At their 1988 party conference a meeting was organized by the Campaign For Real Education which opposes the teaching of sociology, peace studies, world studies, political education, and anti-racist or anti-sexist initiatives (Surkes, 1988).

Overall, there has been, over the past 30 years, an uneasy political resistance to the acceptance of non-white ethnic minorities as equal citizens whose cultures and histories should be respected, but who are also part of the British nation. Politicians prefer to present minorities as scapegoats for social and economic ills, as responsible for inner city decline and problems of law and order. Few public figures have been willing to take a lead in asserting that ethnic minorities do share a British national identity.[3] In this climate it is unsurprising that multicultural educational change in white areas has been so slow, and that a resistance to change is developing which can be described as an educational nationalism.

Educational nationalism
Educational Nationalism is a developing ideological and policy orientation of the late 1980s and possibly the 1990s to the presence of

ethnic minorities in the education system, and a defence of the monocultural values underpinning this system. Over the past 30 years, educational policy responses have variously been described as assimilationist, integrationist and culturally plural, and it is tempting to regard educational nationalism as simply a white backlash against the complex ideas of cultural and democratic pluralism (see Banks and Lynch, 1986). However, educational nationalism depends on the myth that minorities have complete choice and full opportunity to assimilate into the British way of life and British culture – 'The responsibility for the adaptations and adjustments involved in settling in a new country lies entirely with those who have come here to settle and raise families of their own free will' (Honeyford, 1982). Within this view, minorities can only be blamed for their own intransigence if they fail to adapt and adjust.

Educational resistance towards making changes in a system designed for a white majority has, over the past 30 years, illustrated the hypocritical position suggested by Dench (1986). Thus minorities are urged that the most appropriate way for them to achieve equality of opportunity and acceptance into the nation, is to give up adherence to their own culture, language, customs and values and regard themselves as British, adhering to British values. At the same time the white majority, including pupils, parents and some teachers, remain hostile to or suspicious of, the actual presence as well as the cultures of minorities and deny them entry to the idea of a 'nation'. Assimilation or integration, although urged onto minorities, is impossible in a society where the majority culture includes political and cultural beliefs in white superiority, and condones racial discrimination and harassment. Educational nationalists deny that there are barriers placed in the way of minorities to prevent them from achieving educational credentials and training, other than those they create for themselves by inertia, unreasonable demands, lack of fluency in English, or a desire to hold on to their own cultures. Signs of this nationalism are evident in the wide media coverage given to conservative academics and practioners who argue that minorities should abandon demands for their children to be respected as different but equal potential citizens, and should accept colour-blind, monocultural and monolingual policies.

Educational nationalism also depends on a mythologized British heritage and culture, which is assumed to be monolithic and shared by all white individuals with no divisions by class or gender. It is built around an opposition to curriculum change or innovation which would present the British heritage and culture in a different light. History, geography, literature, religious education and social studies are singled out as subjects to remain British-oriented, while world studies, peace studies, social and life skills, sociology and political education are considered to be irrelevant subjects which should be abandoned (Hillgate Group, 1986). This kind of nationalism requires a belief that

> a child brought up in the British way of doing things is encouraged to question and to criticise, to seek fair play and impartial judgement, and to receive as a doctrine only that which he has independent reason to believe to be true. A child brought up in such a culture does not need the presentation of 'alternatives' which so many educationists wish to foist on him.
>
> (Scruton, 1986, p. 132)

Scruton, who has made numerous scholarly right-wing contributions to political and educational nationalism in the 1980s, particularly as the editor of the *Salisbury Review*, undoubtedly represents the views of many people, for whom the superiority of the 'British way of doing things' is beyond question. Educational nationalist views are clearly articulated in the publications of the conservative Hillgate Group (1986, 1987). This group is particularly concerned that the educational establishment has allowed the development of a multicultural curriculum which they consider works against 'the traditional values of Western society' (Hillgate, 1987, p. 3). They oppose the recommendations of the Swann Committee on the grounds that it 'engages our post-colonial guilt feelings and threatens to destroy altogether the basis of our national culture' (p. 4).

The development of educational nationalism has relied on its proponents attacking *all* supporters of cultural pluralism, curriculum change, educational policies for minorities, and all varieties of multicultural, anti-racist education as being politically motivated and likely to be subversive. Honeyford, the Bradford ex-headteacher whose views have been given wide media coverage, has during the 1980s helped to make resistance to pluralism, and educational change for the majority, both educationally and politically respectable. In articles in the *Salisbury Review* in 1983 and 1984 he suggested that those advocating change were likely to be left-wing agitators, and used derogatory stereotypes of minorities to suggest that educational demands by minorities were suspect. He linked those who supported multicultural or anti-racist education to 'a hard core of left-wing political extremists' (Honeyford, 1983) and suggested that 'much of the pressure for a multicultural curriculum comes from the vehement radical left and black organisations' (Honeyford, 1984). His articles, as Halstead has noted (1988) are, for someone who writes about 'British traditions of civilised discourse and good natured tolerance', largely negative about minorities and contain a 'significant core of insulting statements'. Asians are portrayed as given to diatribes which reflect 'the hysterical political temperament of the Indian sub-continent' and West Indians portrayed as lacking in educational ambition (Halstead, p. 69). In 1987 Honeyford called for a public referendum on multicultural education to check the 'powerful multicultural and anti-racist lobby supported by Swann', and in 1988 produced a book which attacked an astonishing collection of individuals and institutions who had apparently misguidedly accepted the proposition that Britain was a racist society. These included 'the Labour, Liberal and SDP parties, all left-wing local councils and some conservative ones, the BBC and the IBA, many trade unions and certain departments of state, notably the Home Office and the DES, as well as sections of the printed media, (Honeyford, 1988, p. 123). Supporters of educational nationalism have been particularly concerned to link multicultural and anti-racist activity (including the work of the Swann Committee) to left-wing politics, and to suggest that it is the imposition of an alien philosophy – which has no popular mandate – onto a British nation, which is being unfairly denigrated. Baroness Cox who particularly influenced the 1988 Education Act towards a predominantly Christian orientation, has suggested that some anti-racist teaching materials are simply 'propaganda designed to undermine our society by dishonest intellectual tactics and promote disaffection and conflict' (Cox, 1986, p. 80). Pearce, a Monday Club member, has argued that the Swann Committee wished to impose a fundamental change in the national culture regardless of national opinion. To him the crucial question is whether an indigenous British culture will maintain its predominance, as 'the native British have a right to preserve their way of life and this must mean that it is their culture which predominates in school.' (1986, p. 141). Pearce considers that pluralism has become a cover for left-wing ideas and that the Swann report is 'brazen, anti-democratic and illiberal' in advocating educational change for the majority. Savery, a Bristol teacher (1987), has adopted the political metaphor of the enemy within to suggest that anti-racist educational activities are 'the instrument of a neo-colonialist minority who seek domination over our domestic territories and who wish to destroy forever the culture that has grown and flourished there'. Then in 1988 Lewis, a leader-writer on the *Daily Mail*, misrepresented the conclusions of the Swann report: 'the materials taught in all subjects are to be in accordance with the values of a multiracial society and to the detriment of British patriotic pride' (Lewis, 1988, p. 142) and went on to conclude that 'the Swann report was a dismal failure' (p. 110).

Opposition to multicultural or anti-racist education or a changed education for all has thus centred around an educational nationalism whose parameters have been defined as a defence of the nations heritage and culture against supposed left-wing, black or minority attack. In addition to political and academic proponents of this view, there are a number of right-wing educational organizations, including parents' groups, who are opposed to any change in a multicultural direction (see Hempel, 1988) and who in addition present any such changes as inevitably leading to an erosion of educational standards for both majority and minority pupils.

A developing educational nationalism can also be observed at the local authority level. Although the majority of local education authorities are now committed to some form of educational change for a multi-ethnic society, some may be encouraged by changes in political control, or by lobbies of interest groups, to abandon multicultural policies and practices. Berkshire LEA made such an attempt in 1987. Although this LEA was one of the first to produce a much-admired and much copied policy on *Education for Racial Equality*, the local council decided to withdraw the policy and substitute new guidelines which reinstated an unproblematic view of a British heritage, and denied a place for minority views and cultures in the curriculum. Thus the new guidelines noted that

> Britain needs to maintain its individuality of culture and heritage in a world bound ever closer by the speed of communication. People from many nations have come to live in this country. In coming to regard it as their own, we want them to share our pride in our indigenous heritage. . . . Some feel we are in danger of losing our British heritage, background and national pride and we do not intend to go down this road in Berkshire. Our textbooks and displays, the general ethos of our schools and colleges, all that we do should reflect a reasonable pride in our nation and things British.
>
> (Berkshire, 1987)

The range of opposition to this plan included the Berkshire Secondary Heads Association, the Berkshire Federation of Primary Heads, the local and national Union of Teachers, the Church of England Board of Education, all the faith centres and minority group organizations in the county, the Commission for Racial Equality and a number of academics and educationalists outside the county. Support was more muted but Honeyford wrote to the *Times Educational Supplement* applauding Berkshire's 'brave decision' to end the 'anti-racist nightmare' in the county. In this instance the county decided to retain its original policy, but other LEAs may decide to rescind or not develop their policies, and schools which opt-out from local authority control will not in future be bound by multicultural policies or changes. Educational nationalism may thus become the favoured ideological policy orientation, rather than any educational change labelled multicultural, anti-racist or even an 'education for all'.

Economics and the national identity

There is undoubtedly considerable resistance on the part of many white British people and their political leaders, to the inclusion of non-white minorities as part of the British nation, and a rejection of the incorporation of minority cultures as part of a British way of life. There is also a strong tendency (see Rex and Tomlinson, 1979) to use minorities as scapegoats for economic and social problems. The majority also tend to consider the reactions of minorities to discrimination and racism as confirming majority views that it is the minorities who are, or who create, the problems. This resistance is paralleled by a reluctance to regard modern Britain as an equal, not a superior, participant in an interdependent world. Since resistance and rejection, and the hypocritical demands on minorities described by Dench (1986) seem perfectly reasonable to many people, the onus is on supporters of democratic pluralism to make out a case for change, and the likely consequences of refusing to acknowledge that minorities are part of the nation and the nation part of an interdependent world.

The proponents of change have usually based their case on humanitarian, moral and social grounds, appealing to the liberal values of equality and justice to which democratic societies subscribe, or noting the likely consequences for social order if minorities do not feel included in the nation. Proponents of change have stressed that an acceptance of cultural pluralism, and a removal of discrimination and institutional racism are necessary to guarantee human and citizenship rights in a democratic society (Dummett, 1983; Banks, 1986). Those investigating the social disorders of the 1980s in British cities have pointed to the possibility of further disorders if minorities are not treated equally as part of the society (Scarman, 1982) or have suggested (Gilroy, 1987, p. 243) that young people in minority groups may retreat into an alternative identity within the territorial boundaries of an urban community if they are not made to feel part of the nation.

However, the strongest arguments for changed views towards minorities at home and towards foreigners overseas may yet turn out to be economic. When the Swann Committee wrote that all pupils should have an increased awareness of the mutual interdependence of nations, it was suggesting a future economic situation in which Britain could no longer afford to assume attitudes of superiority towards people and countries whose trade, investment and factories provide the British with work and a livelihood. The emergence of new, highly technological, industrialized countries, the introduction of new products and the greater number of participants in international trade demonstrate global linkages in which Britain is a partner, not a dominant force, despite the strengths of post-imperial trade links. For example, Nigeria and Saudi Arabia are among the top ten countries receiving British products, and Japan is the fourth largest British trading partner.

Economists have debated whether the growth of multinational corporations would make the nation-state obsolete (Kindleberger, 1970), but this has not happened, there is instead an increased interdependence of the world economy from which British workers benefit. When, for example, the Shanghai bank owns a large number of shares in the Midland Bank, and when Japan's Nissan and Kuwatisu factories employ white workers in the north-east of England, it is economically undesirable to hold imperial stereotypes of 'slitty-eyed Chinese' or the 'yellow peril'. The provision of jobs for British people by the direct foreign investment of countries who would formerly have simply provided an export market for British goods is a new economic reality. The global economy now operates on principles of mutual investment and joint ventures between countries (Bhagwati and Ruggie, 1984) and the majority of these countries involved are not 'white' countries.

A further economic carrot to encourage changed views of minorities in Britain is that currently over 40 per cent of ethnic minorities are under the age of 15, and they will form a sizeable proportion of the potential workforce well into the twenty-first century. As a smaller workforce will be supporting a large number of senior citizens, the trained labour of ethnic minorities alongside the white majority will be urgently needed. It may now be worthwhile for proponents of a multi-ethnic Britain and a changed national identity to move away from the repetitious deploring of racism, to stressing the economic benefits of abandoning superior, hostile, or arrogant attitudes towards non-white minorities both in Britain and abroad. Economic self-interest may be a more powerful force in challenging monocultural, racist beliefs, than moral exhortation or social theats.

Summary
This chapter has suggested that while supporters of educational change for all pupils in a multi-ethnic society have been engaged in description and prescription and in 'multi' versus 'anti' debates, they have ignored the question of national identity. This has allowed opponents of such changes – influential politicians and educationalists – to define the parameters of an opposing debate in terms of a populist educational

nationalism. The arguments have suggested that cultural pluralism threatens a British heritage and culture, and that proponents of change are likely at best to be misguided, and at worst, to be left-wing subversives. Debate on the meaning of a post-imperial national identity and how a re-examined British heritage and culture should be passed on in education is crucial in multi-ethnic Britain. But neo-Victorian beliefs in white racial and cultural superiority, derogatory views of minorities and hypocritical demands that they should abandon their cultures while being denied access to full British nationhood do not advance the debate. The chapter has suggested that while supporters of educational change have previously based their arguments on egalitarianism, human rights and morality or the need for social order, economic arguments might eventually prove more powerful in challenging monocultural and racist views of a British national identity.

Notes

1   This book does not enter into debates about 'what is' a racial, or ethnic group and how such groups are determined by physical or cultural characteristics. The reader is referred to chapter one of Rex, J. (1986), *Race and Ethnicity*. Rex considers that what are called racial or ethnic groups have characteristics imputed to them by others. Physical or cultural characteristics do not determine membership of a racial or ethnic group; it is the behaviour and attitudes of others *towards* these characteristics that determines whether a group is described as racial or ethnic. Minority groups defined as either racial or ethnic can be subject to discrimination and oppression on the basis of their attributed characteristics.

2   Mrs Thatcher's speech to a Conservative rally at Cheltenham on 3 July 1982 included the following remarks:

> There were those who would not admit it . . . but had their secret fears that it was true, . . . that Britain was no longer the nation that had built an Empire and ruled a quarter of the World. Well they were wrong . . . Britain had to be threatened by foreign soldiers and British territory invaded and then the response was incomparable.

> The lesson of the Falklands is that Britain has not changed and this nation still has those sterling qualities which shine through our history.

3   Church leaders in Britain have constituted a leadership in protesting about the exclusion of ethnic minorities from equal citizenship (Faith in the City, 1985).

2 Education for white superiority

> Every school and college has an important role to play in educating children and young people for life in a pluralist society. . . , racially mixed schools have changed most and white schools least. Yet. . . it is the attitude of young white people emerging from white schools that will tell us most about the success of our search for justice and equality.
>
> (Derbyshire County Council, 1987, p. 6)

Despite a re-structuring of education in post-war Britain, there were initially few challenges to its underlying colonial-imperial value base, which supported beliefs in the superiority of white people and white social institutions. In 1952 an organization called 'Racial Unity' was founded to support the United Nations Declaration of Human Rights and to work for justice and equality between racial and ethnic groups. Supporters of this organization regarded education as a crucial instrument in achieving these goals. The school curriculum was singled out as presenting a distorted and inadequate image of non-whites, so that 'young people form a false picture and have a fallacious belief that the white races are inherently superior to all others, and are permanently higher in the scale of humanity' (Racial Unity, 1954). Racial Unity suggested that the education white pupils received was imbued with out-dated racial beliefs, imperial nostalgia, misinformation about colonial peoples – and in the 1950s – already influenced by the emergent anti-immigration lobby. Education for white pupils could not be otherwise than an education for white superiority.

This chapter examines evidence which suggests that over 40 years after the Declaration of Human Rights, there has been remarkably little change in the beliefs that white pupils, parents and some teachers hold, about non-white former colonial settlers in Britain, and about former colonies and the Third World. The limited multicultural and anti-racist initiatives for white pupils implemented since the 1970s so far appear to have made little impact in white areas.

Nationalist themes
Chapter 1 discussed the way in which a narrow concept of nationalism,

supported by influential politicians, public figures and some academics and educationalists, has linked together ideas of the nation and its supposed heritage and culture in ways that exclude ethnic minorities; and how an educational nationalism has presented the curriculum as under attack from multicultural developments. The populist political and cultural beliefs – that racial and ethnic minorities and their cultures have a questionable place in the nation, and that a democratic pluralist society is neither possible nor desirable and should not be encouraged by educational change – are reflected in white schools and in the views of pupils, teachers and parents. The views of pupils in white areas appear to reflect a range of attitudes towards minorities, but with an emphasis on negative evaluation, and displaying a good deal of antagonism, hostility and xenophobia. However, there is also evidence of a recognition of the unfairness of discrimination and antagonism to non-whites, and a limited fraternalist desire for more knowledge of minorities. Rather than simply describing the young people's beliefs as racist and expressing moral condemnation of the xenophobia and arrogance of some of the views expressed, there is a need to distinguish the various beliefs expressed and examine possible reasons for their strengths and persistence. On a very general level, the Swann Committee (DES, 1985a) and others have noted the way in which pupils' hostile beliefs are nurtured in the home and either supported, or not contradicted, by parents, some schools, the media and other wider social and political forces. The following table of the themes occurring in white pupils' statements about ethnic minorities, has been extracted from evidence collected in the 1970s and 1980s from white pupils via essays and class discussions and from data on all-white schools presented to the Swann Committee.

Table 1. *White pupils' views of ethnic minorities: Negative themes*

Exclusionary themes:	*Britain is a 'white' country. Blacks, Asians, foreigners are alien, do not belong, overrun us, do not exist in some areas, should not inter-marry*
Ethnocentric themes:	*Our culture and heritage are superior. Other cultures are strange, exotic, noisy and smelly*
Imperial regret themes:	*'We' once owned the world. The blacks demanded independence*
Scapegoating themes:	*Blacks, Asians and foreigners take 'our' jobs, houses, shops, social security, media, opportunities, and also live in 'luxury' and create urban decay*
Repatriation themes:	*Blacks, Asians, foreigners and illegal immigrants should return or be sent back to their 'own' country*
Racial strife themes:	*Minorities blamed for confrontation and a militant response to racial hostility, also blamed for crime and violence.*

However, there is also evidence of more positive themes emerging from white pupils' views. The positive views are in many instances grudging, paternalistic and hard for the young white people to articulate. They are also often in conflict with parental views. However, it is these kind of positive views that teachers who wish to make changes will have to build upon and reinforce.

Table 2. *White pupils' views of ethnic minorities: Positive themes*

Acceptance themes:	*Minorities, blacks, Asians, Irish have been here a long time. No different to us in many ways*
Sympathy themes:	*Minorities do have problems in Britain. The Third World has problems with drought and famine*
Respect themes:	*Cultural respect for black music and black sportsmen and women; some respect for minority arts and literature.*
Unfairness themes:	*Unfair that minorities are the recipients of name-calling, harassment and violence. Distancing of 'us' from National Front movement and 'real' racists*

The views of white pupils do, on occasion, display an attitudinal paradox (Jeffcoate, 1979, p. 19). Young whites can hold seemingly incompatible positions of acceptance and rejection – for example, the child who has a black best friend, but believes all blacks should be 'sent home'. Feelings of tolerance, fraternalism and egalitarianism can co-exist with prejudice, stereotyping and rejection. Allport, in his studies of prejudice in the USA, noted this paradox and described it as 'the peculiar double-think appropriate to prejudice in a democracy.' (Allport, 1954, p. 19). Contradictory views of ethnic minorities may also be reflecting Dench's (1986) idea of systematic hypocrisy. Dench does not agree that there is any paradox in national majorities holding liberal views on friendship and integration while simultaneously holding discriminatory and rejectionist views. Hypocrisy is simply the norm in democratic societies that wish to be known for their values of progressive tolerance while actually practising discrimination and condoning racism.

Those who are committed to education for all in a multi-ethnic society do have to identify and build on positive attitudes and views. White pupils may be socialized into holding negative and stereotyped views about minorities, but they are also socialized into democratic notions of fair play, equal rights, tolerance and a degree of fraternalism. There is also some evidence that older pupils are willing and able to question negative parental, social and political views about minorities. The major problem for teachers may be to extend both pupils and parental narrow, nationalistic views and help them to accept that fair play, equal rights and fraternal feelings should be extended to all groups within the nation. The following three sections provide evidence which illustrates the positive and negative pupil views encapsulated in Tables 1 and 2. The Swann data also provides some evidence of school, teacher, parental and community views on minorities and on curriculum changes, in white areas. The evidence is predominantly small-scale, qualitative and localized. There has been no large-scale funded survey of white pupil, parent or teacher attitudes towards, and knowledge about, ethnic minorities in Britain.

White views – the 1970s

By the early 1970s some educators were taking the view that the changes that had taken place in the composition of British society ought to be reflected in the school curriculum, but there was little agreement as to how this should happen, and whether schools in 'non-multi-racial areas' would respond to the suggestion that 'curriculum change is of equal relevance in Harrogate or Bournemouth as it is in Handsworth or Brixton' (Townsend and Brittan, 1973, p. 7). In 1972 the Schools Council funded a survey of schools in both multiracial and non-multiracial areas, as a preliminary to a curriculum project to produce materials for use by all pupils in multiracial Britain. Townsend and Brittan, who carried out the survey, received postal information from 58 primary and 68 secondary schools in all-white areas. Over two-thirds of the schools agreed that the curriculum should aim to prepare all pupils for life in a multiracial society, although some headteachers took a strong assimilationist line, and one wrote that 'I do not consider it the responsibility of the English state school to cater for the development of cultures and customs of a foreign nature.' (Townsend and Brittan, 1973, p. 13.) The schools did not necessarily put this aim into practice however – only 29 per cent gave actual examples of changes in the curriculum and many appeared to assume that change would 'just happen' without any action. 'Teaching tolerance' and Oxfam and Shelter projects were mentioned, although there was also evidence of some sophisticated work on race, prejudice and deprivation (*op. cit.*, p. 23). Townsend and Brittan were optimistic that declared support for the preparation of all pupils for life in a multiracial society had given a 'green light' (*op. cit.*, p. 84) to curriculum developers, but the subsequent project 'Education for a Multiracial Society' met considerable resistance. By the time Little and Willey came to survey current provision in all LEAs in relation to education for what was described by them as a multiethnic society, they found a general view in white areas that the 'wider multi-ethnic society has little relevance in their schools' (Little and Willey, 1981, p. 10) and that 'little has been done to give children in schools with few or no ethnic minority pupils a positive awareness of cultural diversity' (Willey, 1984, p. 39).

The Schools Council Curriculum Project provided some of the first evidence of white pupils' ignorance about, and hostility to, those regarded as racially, ethnically and culturally different. Pupils' views illustrated the nationalistic themes described in the previous section, particularly towards 'blacks and Pakis' in Britain, foreigners and the Third World overseas (Jeffcoate, 1979). Jeffcoate, with other workers on this project, also provided evidence of teacher beliefs that children did not notice racial differences and that race was not an issue in white schools. These beliefs were strongly held despite the presentation of evidence that children do develop racial awareness as early as three, and can form negative views of racial groups considered to be inferior by the age of five (Jeffcoate, 1979; *New Society*, 1978).

The Schools Council Project workers found that they had to develop strategies to demonstrate to teachers that their pupils did indeed hold derogatory and stereotyped views about minorities. One Head of a white school was encouraged to play a balloon game with a class of top juniors, inviting them to write about landing, in a balloon, in a country they did not want to visit. Top of the list of rejected countries was Africa, where Tarzan images of hostile natives brandishing spears mixed with Oxfam images of poverty and disease (Jeffcoate, 1979, p. 16). The Head also held discussions to dispel ignorance about Asians in Britain. Essays subsequently produced by the children contained mixtures of fact and error, 55 million people in Britain being translated in 55 million immigrants. Exclusionist, repatriation and scapegoating themes loomed large in the children's work.

> I think it is not right for black people to come and take our shops and things . . . they are trying to take over the country.
>
> (p. 20)

> England is meant for whites, (blacks) should be thrown out. Whites invented telly so only whites should go on telly.
>
> (p. 20)

Teachers' assumptions that race was not an issue and 'did not affect us as our children never see anyone different', were contradicted by the hostile reactions of the white pupils. Nursery and infant school teachers in particular, reported their surprise at infant antagonisms to pictures depicting black people. One teacher presented photographs to a group of four-year-old children, using a traditional teaching method. The children made no reference to skin colour or race. She then presented the photographs to a second group of children without saying anything at all. Gradually the children responded with a chant of 'Ugh! Blackies', punctuated by noises of disgust and derision (*New Society*, 1978, p. 367). This project produced a report which was vetoed for publication by the Schools Council's own programme committee. The General Secretary of the National Union of Teachers, who was a member of the programme committee, defended this decision in a series of letters to the *Times Educational Supplement*, denying that the veto was made 'out of a desire to cover up the attitudes of pupils or teachers on racialism and race relations' (Jarvis, 24.2.78). The report was eventually published in an edited version (Schools Council, 1981).

Jeffcoate (1979) also reported receiving essays from his white pupils on the subject of 'Immigrants'. In these essays exclusionary, scapegoating, and repatriation themes were joined by those of imperial regret. One girl wrote:

> At one time we owned nearly all the world but now we've only got a little piece. There are too many coloureds in our country.
>
> (Jeffcoate, 1979, p. 99)

Scapegoating themes, blaming immigrants for shortages of jobs, houses and health care and for taking resources, and opportunities from whites, were very evident, and were embellished with quotations culled from stories in the popular press.

> They come from Pakistan to have operations on the National 'ealth.
>
> (p. 99)

The theme of repatriation was supported by the idea that illegal immigration was commonplace.

Jeffcoate's work fuelled a debate on strategies for combatting white pupil racial hostility, but this debate was, in the 1970s, confined to multiracial schools. He considered that the antagonisms displayed by white pupils who had found a ready scapegoat for social and urban problems could not simply be dealt with by a moral condemnation – what Rex has described as 'preaching at skinheads' (Rex, 1981) and he advocated allowing white pupils' hostile views to be voiced and discussed in the classroom (see Jeffcoate, 1979, 1984; Gaine, 1987). In the 1980s strategies for dealing with overt racial hostility in white schools and colleges are still largely a matter of trial and error (Taylor, 1987a; Troyna and Selman, 1988).

White Views – the 1980s

Throughout the 1980s, evidence has suggested that white pupils' hostility and antagonism to those perceived as racially and culturally different, has increased rather than decreased. *British Social Attitudes*

(1984) noted the paradox that while officially Britain is a society devoted to racial equality and tolerance, the proportion of people prepared to describe themselves as racially prejudiced has actually risen. A survey of young people undertaken for *New Society* in 1986 found that 42 per cent of white pupils up to 19 years of age said they were prejudiced against other races, Asians being the most likely recipients of prejudice (Williams, 1986). It may be that, taking a cue from their political leaders, young white people now feel freer to admit to racial antagonism. Rex and Tomlinson noted in 1979 that views about racial minorities, which would have been regarded as morally disgraceful in the 1950s, had become accepted assumptions by the 1970s (Rex and Tomlinson, 1979). In addition, the presentation of young blacks as responsible for the inner city disturbances in the 1980s, and jingoistic attitudes expressed freely during the 1982 Falklands war, may have encouraged young people to become more nationalistic and exclusive.

The antagonistic racial views of young white people, documented in the limited research evidence, are however those of ordinary white pupils, who are often eager to dissociate themselves from extremist neo-Fascist groups in Britain. They represent the views of ordinary school pupils whose parents and families span the social class hierarchy and the range of political affiliations. This same point was made by the Commission for Racial Equality (1987) in discussing the harassment of ethnic minority pupils in multiracial schools. It is not simply a lunatic fringe, who hold negative or antagonistic views about minorities, it is ordinary white pupils, students, parents and teachers. Extremist movements such as the National Front and the British Movement have not been slow to recognize the potential for recruitment in white areas (see Durham, 1986) and many schools in these areas suggest there is National Front influence on pupils (see DES, 1985a, pp. 243–314). But it is important to recognize that these movements capitalize on the antagonistic beliefs already present in white areas.

Nevertheless, many teachers in the mid-1980s still found difficulty in admitting that a major response of white pupils towards racial minorities, whether they are present in the area or not, is one of hostility and unwillingness to concede the rights of equal citizenship. In the north-east of England, Mould, an LEA advisor, tested the degree of white pupils' empathy with black people to convince teachers of the extent of racism in schools (Mould 1986). Heads, teachers and administrators took the view that children in the area were not racist, regarded all pupils as equal and that the area had no problems. Three hundred Tyneside pupils attending three secondary, two primary and one special school, wrote essays on the subject of black people. Mould's analysis of the views expressed by the white pupils surprised and disturbed the teachers: 75 per cent of the children held negative attitudes towards black people, 25 per cent of whom held strongly hostile views. There were no significant variations between essays by girls and boys and by special school pupils. An exclusive nationalist theme was most evident – 'almost all the children spoke of Britain as a white society' (Mould, 1986, p. 9). The repatriation theme was very evident, and the scapegoating theme included the belief that far from being disadvantaged, Asians and Africans 'lived in luxury' and should be blamed for any material success they had achieved.

'Black people have been in our country for a long time and most come from Africa. They started taking our jobs and making the British unemployed. I think anyone who even looks black should be deported.'

'I think the Pakis steal jobs from the English.'

'I think coloured people who are from different countries . . . should be chucked out of our country . . . most coloured people are richer than us, they have Mercedes, Rolls Royces and big detached bungalows.'

'Soon we'll have all Africa over here ruling us.'

(*op. cit.*, p. 10)

Asians, collectively described as Pakistani or Paki, were the target for the most hostile pupil criticism, Asian shop-keepers invoking particular antagonism, perhaps because the pupils most frequently come into contact with Asian shop-keepers and market traders.

Positive views towards minorities were also evident in Mould's study, although paternalistic and confused. The themes of acceptance, the unfairness of name-calling and of disapproval of inter-marriage, of threats from skinheads and the National Front, and the 'cruel and unfair' treatment of a black footballer who had banana skins thrown at him during a match, were all mentioned (Mould, *op. cit.*, p. 11). Mould concluded that despite some positive views, her exercise had supported the findings of the Swann Committee of widespread racism, patronizing and stereotyped ideas about minorities, ignorance of their actual cultural backgrounds or life-style, and lack of knowledge of facts about race and migration.

Mould's exercise was repeated a year later in work on the first Master's level degree course in multicultural education to be offered in an English Institution of Higher Education.[1] Thirty-seven essays by 13- and 14-year-old comprehensive school pupils were analysed. Seventeen of the essays expressed intolerant and negative views illustrating the familiar nationalistic themes. The pupils' own experiences were often reflected in their writing and suggested fears and insecurity and an inability to deal with those regarded as social or cultural inferiors. One girl began her essay:

'I don't mind black people in Britain but I can't stand Pakistanis. They are the rudest people I've ever known . . . the reason I can't stand them is because they think they rule our country.'

She followed this with a detailed description of an encounter with a market stall holder and continued:

'They mumble away in their own language. The money they must make by keeping all those pennies must give them a big profit, as if they didn't have enough money. Nearly all the shops in north Tyneside are run by Pakis and Indians. They parade around in their stupid saris and turbans stinking the area out with smells of curry and Paki smells.'

Another essay stressed the 'trouble' caused by black people, on the racial strife theme.

'Black people cause crime and are on drugs. They cause trouble by setting off bombs.'

On a more positive note, 14 of the essays expressed some views which were tolerant and signified some understanding of the position of minorities. The unfairness of name-calling and of differential treatment because of skin-colour were particularly noted.

'I've nothing against black people because they haven't done anything to us. Some black people are really nice but sometimes they get called names like wog. They are just like us but with a different coloured skin. I really feel sorry for them when they get called when they haven't done anything to us.'

Positive views included an awareness of unfair job descrimination and dislike of the unjustified violence directed against minorities. One essay referred to the 'common humanity' of black and white and several essays used the Tyneside dialect to refer to black friends as 'really canny'.

Overall, the views expressed by pupils in the North East in the mid-1980s provided depressing evidence that schools had not yet begun to find ways of offering an appropriate education for white pupils.

The white pupils laid particular stress on the importance of name-calling, by either using derogatory names, or deploring the unfairness of name-calling. While general name-calling has always been common in schools, there has undoubtedly been an increase in the use of derogatory racial and ethnic names, most of which are directed against racial and cultural minorities. Elinor Kelly, who was commissioned by the MacDonald Committee of Enquiry[2] into the murder of an Asian boy by a white boy in 1986 in Manchester (Kelly and Cohen, 1988), undertook a survey to determine the extent of racial name-calling and how this affected inter-racial behaviour. She surveyed 902 pupils in three Manchester schools in 1987, the pupils completing a questionnaire about their own experiences of name-calling and fighting. The results of her survey provided 'unambiguous and disturbing evidence of the reality of racist behaviour in our schools, evidence that cannot be rationalised away by the critics of anti-racist strategies.' (Kelly and Cohen, 1988, p. 4.) A list of the racial and ethnic names Kelly found were currently used in schools is appended to this chapter to offer some idea of the extent of racial and ethnic labelling.

Racial name-calling was also documented as a problem in Norwich by Akhtar and Stronach (1986) despite the city being a place where 'ethnic minorities are a barely acknowledged presence' (p. 23). Akhtar's study found that the few Asian pupils in Norwich schools faced considerable racial abuse from white pupils, one little boy reporting that he was called 'second-hand, toilet paper, and chocolate and bloody Asian.' Teachers adopted evasive strategies to deny there was a problem despite the evidence. One strategy was simply to assert that 'children accept each other', another to assert that there was a problem but it was not racial – 'all children fight at times' – and a third strategy was to recognize a racial problem but deny that it was serious. Teachers used moral appeals for tolerance which did not appear to be effective. This study also noted that Asian parents were sometimes keen to collude with teachers and play down the racist implications of name-calling. This response by minority parents has been noted by workers on the Education Support Grant projects described in this book.[3]

Gaine (1987) has documented similar negative views and reactions from pupils in southern schools, and has noted that the views indicated a complete ignorance of colonial history, much geographical and political confusion, cultural ignorance – particularly over world religions and Asian languages – and patterned, rather than chance, misinformation. His pupils, who wrote essays on 'Black and Coloured People in Britain', provided some evidence of good intentions towards minorities combined with the confused bigotry of nationalistic themes. Thus, one girl began her essay with the positive sentiment that:

> I think having black and coloured people in England is fantastic. I think we should mix together.

But she ended her essay on the repatriation theme of:

> Why don't they go back to their own country.

> (Gaine, 1987, p. 6)

Another pupil expressed both a scapegoating theme, a distinct cultural ethnocentricity and perhaps a need for comparative religious education in his essay:

> I think black and coloured people are taking our jobs. The Pakistanis wear turbans for a religion, and they bang their heads against a big wall and kiss the wall and they smell.

(op. cit., p. 7)

Gaine noted that the mixture of confused beliefs, nationalistic solutions to the perceived problems of a black presence, and cultural and historical ignorance cannot conceivably be the product of first-hand experience of the white pupils. Chapter three of this book suggests that at least some of the curious beliefs and misinformation is a product of out-dated imperial values which still underpin much of the school curriculum. Gaine agrees that whatever the genesis of pupils' current views and beliefs, it is the school curriculum which must be the target for change.

> 'Pupils are misinformed and intolerant about many things, but . . . they are not just misinformed but dangerously so. If anyone means it when they say Britain is a multicultural society then these comments, highly typical of white British children, have to be taken as giving clear imperatives for the curriculum.'

(Gaine, 1987, p. 9)

The Swann Committee's 'All-white Schools' project

Comprehensive evidence of the attitudes and views of teachers and pupils in white schools towards ethnic minorities, was provided for the Swann Committee by Matthews and Fallon. These two advisors undertook to provide case studies of all-white schools or those with very few ethnic minority pupils. During the winter of 1982/3 they visited 26 schools in six Local Authorities, three in the north of England and three in the South. The schools visited were primary and secondary, county-and voluntary-aided. Following the visits to the schools, Matthews and Fallon met officers of the Local Education Authorities for a discussion of their findings. Reports of the school visits and discussions can be found in the Swann Report (DES, 1985a, pp. 243–314). The reports vividly illustrated the gap between national policy in the early 1980s and exhortation about the need to educate all pupils for life in a multi-ethnic society, and the actual acceptance of this need. The idea that multicultural education had implications for all schools appeared to be rejected by many white schools, who took a narrow and insular view that 'we do not have a multi-ethnic society in this school' (p. 236). This rejection of ethnic minorities as belonging to the whole society, was matched by a widespread racism either unintentional and latent, or overt and aggressive, in many of the schools visited. 'The extent to which myths and stereotypes of ethnic minority groups are established and reinforced by parental attitudes, the influence of the media and through institutional practices within the schools, is, we believe, all too apparent' (DES, 1985a, p. 236).

The concept of being part of a multi-ethnic society was generally not acceptable to the schools, who saw multicultural education as remote or irrelevant to their own localized needs, and any curriculum changes towards recognition of cultural diversity or challenges to racism were regarded as 'too controversial and too inflammatory to contemplate' (p. 236). Teachers were generally found to reflect the attitudes of their local areas and felt they lacked knowledge or confidence to raise multicultural issues, blaming their inadequate training. Their attitude towards ethnic minorities 'ran the whole gamut of racial misunderstanding and folk mythology . . . racial stereotypes were common, and attitudes ranged from the unveiled hostility of a few, through the apathy of many, the condescension of others, to total acceptance and respect by a minority' (p. 236). The Swann Committee concluded that pupils, lacking direct contact with minorities, appeared to be influenced by parents and the local community, who often rejected 'outsiders' *per se*, and by the local press which was often biased against 'immigrants'. The stereotyped and negative presentation of minorities on television was also considered to influence pupils, and the school curriculum was singled out as still contributing to an education for white superiority. History and geography lessons and textbooks which 'emphasised an Anglocentric and Imperialist view of the world as well as portraying developing countries in an outdated manner' (p. 237) were particularly noted.

However, there were indications in white schools that some teachers were willing to re-appraise their own work and wanted clear advice and guidance from the DES and their local authority. The local education authority officers also expressed a desire for guidance in developing and implementing multicultural policies, but were anxious to avoid 'political repercussions'. The most encouraging signs were the number of individual pupils in the school who expressed a desire to learn about ethnic minorities and were willing to challenge the racist attitudes of both their peers and their parents.

The Matthews visits
Matthews visited four schools in Local Education Authority A, four in B and five in C.

'A' was a rural county with very few ethnic minorities. In a white infants' school, children were ignorant about black people born in Britain although they knew that 'some people don't like black people'. On the positive side the pupils were interested in differences between people, and the headteacher wished to develop a curriculum with a moral framework to help pupils understand and tolerate others. In the three co-educational comprehensive schools visited in this area (one a voluntary-aided school) there were more negative than positive views of minorities. At school A2, a white comprehensive, the teachers considered that 'we are lucky – we have few coloureds and no problems of that kind'. Nevertheless they also reported that National Front slogans were written on books and that the parents and local community held bigoted views. In school A4, the teachers reported overt racism among pupils; one teacher's view was that 'in every class some children would pack all the immigrants back home' (DES, 1985a, p. 249). One pupil explained rather apologetically to Matthews that 'it was nothing personal about coloured people' – he just didn't like foreigners at all (p. 250). However, there were also signs of teacher awareness of the need for change in these schools, particularly by the Heads of English, History and Drama. Some gypsy children were accepted at school A2, and an Indian member of staff at A4. School A3, the voluntary-aided school, was interesting in that fourth year pupils, writing essays on 'Race' for Matthews, produced work which was 'extraordinarily free from prejudice and remarkably fair' and a Sikh teacher at the school was held in high regard. In 1983 a multicultural policy was in the planning stages in A but no guidance had been offered to schools at this time by the Authority.

In Local Authority B, another largely rural county but with some minority settlement, particularly an Italian community, there was rather more antagonism to minorities in the schools, In a mainly white infants' school, teachers seemed unaware of the extent of a racial prejudice in both the children and parents, but Matthews found that the children spontaneously claimed that they 'disliked black people'. At school B2, a large comprehensive with a few minority pupils, a multicultural approach to the curriculum was not considered appropriate by most teachers, although they were aware of strong racial prejudice and antipathy to 'foreigners' in the community. One teacher was of the opinion that 'kids have an in-built racial prejudice here' but another was worried that ethnic minorities were given 'favoured treatment'. Twenty fourth-year pupils produced essays for Matthews of which eight were antagonistic to minorities, ten were neutral and two sympathetic. The pupils' ignorance of the numbers of ethnic minority people was 'appalling – estimates ranged from six to twenty million'. Examples of pupil negative comments were:

I think there are too many Pakys and foreigners in our country.

The foreigners take our houses, our jobs, our food and sometimes our women.

You see these Pakys riding round in Rolls Royces and then you see a British family with no car.

There are millions of immigrants from China and Pakistan that speak all different languages, I think they should be chucked out.

(p. 253)

Schools B3 and B4 displayed similar ignorance and prejudices. A teacher in B3 described this as 'a hatred of black skins' (p. 254) and in a recent mock election, the National Front candidate had won third place. In discussions with fifth-year pupils at B4 Matthews noted that 21 out of 30 statements were negative towards black people, including 'We should have listened to Enoch Powell'; 'My grandmother hates blacks' and 'if they are different and don't speak English they must accept aggro' (p. 257). A black Head of Department in B4 had experienced racial harassment both in and out of school. However the schools also demonstrated some positive views of minorities. West Indians were admired for their sporting ability and 'carefree attitude' and the Italian pupils were considered by teachers to be well integrated. The religious education syllabus in the school included World Faiths, with most parents supporting this, and mothers attending an adult education class at one school thought that pupils should meet minorities and experience other cultures. This Local Authority, and Local Authority C, had developed policy statements on race relations in 1982, which had been issued to schools.

Local Authority C was a metropolitan district with some minority settlement, and two of the five schools visited had a number of ethnic minority pupils. An infants' school with a few children of Asian origin had an interested staff who had contacted the National Association for Multiracial Education[4] to help organize in-service training and who expressed a desire to help the white community 'value Asian culture'. The parents Matthews spoke to held negative views of minorities, 'the troubles start when there are too many blacks' and 'it's alright as long as our children are not pushed aside.' At a primary school with about 30 per cent ethnic minority pupils the teachers told Matthews frankly that the local community was racist, the National Front had a strong presence and some of the parents were members. Pupils' racial antagonisms appeared to increase as they progressed through the school. Teachers noted that 'White kids think that Muslims and Hindus are a joke', 'parents call African dance and music "them Paki dances"' and white infant pupils referred to black pupils as 'that chocolate over there'. Despite the minority presence no wall displays depicted minorities, and the pupils were at this time chauvinistic and jingoistic about the Falklands war.

In school C3, a comprehensive with 17 per cent ethnic minority pupils, the Head counted the pupils for Matthews but said he 'didn't particularly want to know' numbers. The staff were aware of 'submerged racism' but did not know how to deal with it (p. 264). Boys in the Upper School were described as 'National Front below the surface'. There appeared to be a view among both staff and pupils that Asian pupils were not welcome in the school or the community and were discriminated against, but that this was 'their own fault' (p. 265). In C4, a comprehensive with few minority pupils, the reactions of staff and pupils were equally depressing and 'racism is admitted by the staff to be rife in the school' (p. 266). There was support for the National Front and the British Movement from parents who handed on their racial antagonisms to their children. One teacher reported that 'Paki bashing was part of the local culture' (p. 266). In C5, a comprehensive with 5 per cent minority pupils, the Head did not think 'Paki' was a defamatory label and 'a significant number of staff did not see what all the fuss was about.' However, the Head of Social Studies reported that she came from a school in a minority area and was greeted by 'nigger lover' on the blackboard, books and materials depicting other cultures were defaced, and a discussion of race in a social studies course was dropped when white pupils reacted in racist terms and staff became frightened (p. 269). The mother of one white girl objected to her daughter 'doing this thing on Pakis' (a CSE project on Asian girls in Britain) and an Indian teacher at the school said he was racially harassed and 'the children still look at me as an alien who is not supposed to be here' (p. 268). On the positive side, there was some sign of awareness of the need for curriculum change to counter pupil and parent hostile racial and cultural views. School C4 had set up a working party to combat racism through curriculum change and report to the LEA, and in all the schools the English and RE departments were working to produce new syllabuses and provide more suitable textbooks.

Reports of these visits were discussed with the Chief Education Officers and others in the local authorities visited. Senior officers remained cautious in their reception of the information on the extent of racial prejudice in the schools, and failure of teachers to adopt strategies or re-orientate the curriculum to cultivate more positive attitudes in the pupils. The elected members in the authorities also could not be convinced of the need for curriculum change in the white schools, although they saw the need for change in multiracial schools.

The Fallon visits

Fallon visited four schools in local authority X, a largely rural area, four schools in Y, a mixed rural and industrial county with some ethnic minority settlement, and four schools and a sixth-form college in Z, another largely rural area. None of these authorities had a formal multicultural policy although X and Y were considering such a development.

In an infants' school in a market town in X, Fallon found that teachers were pre-occupied with local problems and failed to portray the multicultural nature of modern society through the curriculum, reading materials or visual displays. However this school did receive gypsy and travellers' children well, and the school was popular with traveller parents. At X2, a large comprehensive, teachers reported stereotyped and racist views of minorities by the working class parents of 'this insular, cautious community' (p. 282) but still considered that curriculum change was only appropriate in multiracial schools. Fallon found the history syllabus was traditional with a 'very Anglocentric third year study of the British Empire' (p. 280). However, he also found that by the sixth form, pupils were challenging the narrow view of the world which they had previously not questioned, and they were worried that their peers, who had left school, had had no opportunity to do this. The sixth form also felt they had been denied access to political ideas and to knowledge of ethnic minorities, whom they expected to meet in adult life. At X3, a medium-sized comprehensive, teachers also believed that preparation for life in a multicultural society was only relevant to multiracial schools, although a geography teacher reported racist responses when reference was made to Empire or Commonwealth, a chemistry teacher reported a 'nigger hating' attitude in fourth and fifth year pupils, and the Head of History thought that racial prejudice was not diminished by a history syllabus dominated by Western European attitudes. However, as at school X2, fifth- and sixth-year pupils were able to admit that their prejudices were irrational, and expected to work with ethnic minorities after school; also at X3, the Chairman of the Governors was keen to employ ethnic minority teachers. School X4 served an insular community that 'lumps together all coloured people into a stereotyped Paki' and believes that 'coloureds take our jobs' (p. 285). Teachers were concerned at the pupil acceptance of stereotypes of minorities and foreigners in comics and on television and believed that 'parental prejudice was beyond modification'. First-year pupils admitted to name-calling, Prods (Protestants), Pakis and Niggers being the most common. However, Fallon also found that pupils in this school had a 'disposition to fairness' and wished to learn more about ethnic minorities, especially by exchanges with schools in urban areas. A Head of House with adopted West Indian children believed that the younger generation were less prejudiced and more accepting than their parents.

In Local Authority Y, at a large primary school on a council estate, Fallon found that while teachers believed that the pupils did not notice race or colour and 'only' displayed superficial prejudice by name-calling, the children were willing to admit to irrational prejudice. The local community in this area believed that Asian workers had undermined trade union rights and 'perks' and were not inclined to pass on liberal views to their children. The staff at this school however had begun to attend multicultural courses and organize teacher exchanges with multiracial schools. In the three large comprehensive schools visited in Local Education Authority Y, Fallon found a good deal of hostility and prejudice towards minorities and a 'calculated disinterest in issues external to the school'. At Y2 he found strong negative attitudes in a low-ability fifth-year group, who greeted him with 'we've got to talk to you about niggers and wogs and things' (p. 292). The Home Economics teacher reported that a common response to foreign food was that 'it stinks', the RE syllabus ignored comparative religions, and in English 'pupils completely rejected any books portraying black people on the dust cover'. In school Y3, pupils were prejudiced against 'Krauts and Pakis' and keen to 'send them back home' and in Y4, discussion of other cultures and life-styles was often dismissed as 'stupid' by the pupils. There was some evidence in all three schools of a willingness to change on the part of pupils and staff. One pupil told Fallon that his education so far had given him the impression that 'we are British and we are best' (p. 297) and some pupils felt there was ignorance and apathy over contemporary political issues. English, History, Geography and RE teachers were most likely to express anxiety at the limited horizons and misconceptions of pupils and wished to introduce new curriculum content and attend in-service courses.

In rural LEA Z, however, a primary school with only four ethnic minority pupils had been challenged by a Jamaican mother, who had brought multicultural books into the library and mounted an exhibition. She also challenged teachers' views that school could do little against parental attitudes and the influence of television. The junior library of this school contained some out-dated books including a 1964 book describing 'pygmies as resembling monkeys' (p. 298). At Z2, a middle school, Fallon found a very insular closed community suspicious of 'townies, gypsies and tourists'. Third-year pupils expressed the view that 'Blackies take our jobs' and 'the French are dirty people who eat frogs'. However, the staff at this school were working towards a positive focus on multicultural and global issues. In Z3, a smaller upper school, the librarian told Fallon that 'a brown or black face on the cover is enough to prevent pupils choosing the book' (p. 302), but although the staff were paternalistic about ethnic minorities they had begun to attend in-service courses, studied literature debating race issues and were making curriculum changes to help pupils 'learn that goodness, right, dignity and worthiness' is common to much of human-kind' (p. 304). Pupils at school Z4, a secondary modern, and at a neighbouring sixth-form college displayed prejudice and a willingness to stereotype. Fallon found that at the secondary modern school, pupils suffered from feelings of inferiority and insecurity and there was much sexism. Boys stereotyped West Indians, Chinese and Germans (through the influence of televised war films) more than girls, but staff did not know how to combat prejudices. The Head of English worried that books depicting minorities 'would evoke racist fears at present unconsidered' (p. 310) but the History and Geography teachers were concerned about patronizing, colonialist approaches in their subjects and were considering changes. The sixth-form college had been a target for National Front attention, and the Principal had had to forbid the wearing of NF badges. He felt that racial discrimination was 'rife among his extremely conservative students', encouraged by local authority attitudes. He had sent 15 students on a visit to Brixton, but this had intensified their pejudice that 'we are white, this is our country and they should go back where they came from' (p. 310). However, staff at the college were concerned to provide accurate knowledge of other groups locally and globally, and Economics, Sociology and Home Economics courses used material to 'O' and 'A' level which attempted to counter stereotypes. The Deputy Principal had taught in Africa and in multiracial schools and was committed to making appropriate changes in the college.

In discussions with education officers from the three LEAs, Fallon found interest and positive responses from X and Y, although issues and principles of multicultural education in white areas had hitherto not been a consideration. Y was considering appointing an advisor with a wide brief in multicultural concerns. Z believed that multicultural education was beyond its concern and referred Fallon's report to a Head and an advisor who had taught in multiracial schools.

The reports of these visits demonstrated considerable differences between schools and between pupils in the extent of knowledge about, stereotyping of and hostility to, black and minority fellow citizens, and to foreigners. More information on those schools which had managed to create positive feelings towards minorities and on the awareness of

Britain as a multiracial society would have been enlightening. How, for example, had school A3 created its friendly atmosphere 'extra-ordinarily free from prejudice'? The two schools with a large number of minority pupils demonstrated a good deal of antagonism to minority pupils, but these visits by Matthews and Fallon demonstrated beyond question that it is not necessary for minorities to be present for pupils, and in some cases teachers, to hold ignorant, stereotyped and hostile views of those perceived to be racially and culturally different. It also showed that these views can be strongly reinforced by negative parental and community views. The pupil views expressed in this evidence collected for the Swann Committee illustrated the nationalist themes described earlier in this chapter, particularly exclusionist, ethnocentric, scapegoating and repatriation themes. The visits also illustrated the difficulties many teachers experienced in coming to terms with the racial antagonisms and cultural ignorance displayed by some pupils, who were often supported by parents who held similar views. It is perhaps not surprising that, as the Schools Council study found in multiracial schools in the 1970s (*New Society*, 1978) many teachers in white schools in the 1980s preferred to deny, or minimize, the extent of pupil antagonism. Where teachers did recognize the problems they were often genuinely fearful of raising issues which would evoke racist responses, and they did not know how to respond to overt racial hostility expressed by pupils and parents.

White parents

There is no large scale research describing the views of white parents in white areas about ethnic minorities, although there is a variety of interest groups claiming to represent white parental opinion. More comprehensive information on white parental views comes from research on white parents living in multi-ethnic areas whose children attend, or have attended, multi-ethnic schools. The lack of research evidence creates difficulties for educationalists trying to understand the role of parents in socializing their children into particular views of ethnic minorities in Britain.

The large amount of literatue on prejudice and socialization produced in Europe and America has clearly demonstrated that white parents can be extremely influential in socializing their children into negative perceptions of, and hostile behaviour toward, groups regarded as racially or ethnically different (Allport, 1954; Milner, 1983; Davey, 1984; Lynch, 1987), although clearly teaching of such negative views is not confined to white parents in Western societies. But since the pattern of race relations in Britain is still largely one of unequal treatment of, and discrimination against, non-whites, it is not surprising that many white parents rear their children to hold negative or at least neutral views about ethnic minorities in Britain.

There is long standing evidence of white parental antipathy to the education of their children alongside non-white children, and the media publicity given to white parents views in multi-ethnic areas has undoubtedly influenced parents outside these areas, although in the later 1980s some evidence is emerging of the development of more tolerant attitudes among white parents in these areas. In the early 1960s white parents voiced fears that 'their' schools would be 'taken over' by immigrant children and rationalized these fears by claiming that the presence of minority children would lower school standards. Later the rationalization changed to suggest that non-white children were being favoured to the detriment of white children (see Tomlinson, 1984).

More recently, white parental opinion in both multi-ethnic and white areas is being mobilized against a multicultural curriculum which is presented as a threat to a traditional English and Christian environment (Pearce, 1985; Naylor, 1988a). As early as 1963, white parents in Southall protested against the numbers of Asian children entering local schools, and the Minister of Education visited Southall in person to reassure parents that measures were being taken to prevent lowered standards. In effect this meant a recommendation to Parliament that no school should take more than 30 per cent immigration children and that Asian children should be dispersed by bussing (Rose *et al*, 1969). Both these measures turned out to be unworkable. As in the USA, white flight from urban multiracial schools led to 'majority black' schools and bussing was eventually ruled to be racial discrimination.

Throughout the 1970s many white parents remained antagonistic to the idea of their children attending schools with minority pupils. The House of Commons Select Committee on Race Relations and Immigration, collecting evidence for their 1973 report on *Education*, heard evidence in Liverpool of 'white reluctance to send children to a school they regard as having coloured people' (Select Committee, 1973, vol. 3, p. 560). The committee also heard 'some totally nauseating statements from parents' (p. 557) as to why they wanted re-housing away from multiracial schools. One enlightened local councillor, giving evidence of the antagonisms of parents, wanted 'a team of people to go into the all-white areas adjacent to the coloured area and try to tackle their prejudices' (p. 557). This suggestion was not taken up and there has never been any positive educational activity directed towards changing the views of white parents. Some evidence of white ignorance about minority parents was provided by Da Costa

(1988), examining the history of black supplementary schooling in Britain. He recorded that shortly after the Haringey supplementary school had been set up in 1972 white residents called the police after seeing gatherings of black parents delivering and collecting their children. One black parent told Da Costa 'I think they were worried we might be fomenting some kind of insurrection or revolutionary activity . . . they found it difficult to believe that black parents were capable of taking the trouble of organizing a Saturday school' (Da Costa, 1988, p. 149).

In their survey of white parents in Handsworth in the later 1970s, Rex and Tomlinson found that 'among the white parents the feeling was that the presence of black children stigmatized their schools' (Rex and Tomlinson, 1979, p. 194). In attempting to explain white parental antagonisms Rex and Tomlinson concluded that there was a cumulative principle at work whereby racial beliefs stemming from imperialism and the colonial period, were being reinforced by 'racial' events in Britain and by sensational media reporting of such events. Thus, to white parents both in and out of multiracial areas the image of a 'colonial savage' was reinforced by images of police confrontation and violent ghettos. White parents, themselves educated through an ethnocentric curriculum which had often presented non-whites in derogatory or stereotyped ways, and in an economic situation of competition for jobs and housing, were not inclined to want their children educated alongside those whom they had been taught to regard as inferior.

In the early 1980s, further evidence demonstrated that middle as well as working class parents felt a stigma at having their children educated alongside minority children, even on a temporary basis, Richards (1983) reported a Nottinghamshire project which involved an exchange between an inner city junior school and a suburban primary school. The white parents objected to their children mixing with 'these immigrants' from the inner city (p. 223). Chapter six in this book notes that some non-white children on school exchange projects were subject to hostility in white areas, and a report on the London borough of Brent's programme for racial equality in schools, produced in 1988 by Sir David Lane noted that: 'Shortly before my enquiry parties of mainly black children from two Brent schools went on organised visits to Cornwall and the Isle of Wight; they were surprised and shaken to be greeted by racial abuse from some of their rural contemporaries' (Lane, 1988, p. 8). Further evidence of white attitudes in the south-west has been provided by Blair (1988), an Exeter teacher, who has written movingly about the racial abuse of her own children in white schools. She agreed with Rex and Tomlinson

(1979) that the views and behaviour of white parents of all social classes is still conditioned by 'the dying embers of Empire' (Blair, 1988, p. 42) and has noted that it appears very difficult for white Britons to abandon their feelings of innate superiority towards people who have been so recently subjugated and dominated by white Europeans. These feelings are reinforced by beliefs in the original 'primitive lifestyles' of the colonized people, and by the beliefs that those in the former colonies have 'failed to make good the gift of independence'.

White parental views in the 1980s

In the later 1980s, white parental antagonisms have been given wide media publicity, encouraged by the year-long dispute in Dewsbury in the Kirklees local authority. Complaints about lowered school standards have increasingly been linked to developments in multi-cultural education. Multi-ethnic schools which have attempted to take account of the presence of minority pupils, have been falsely presented as denying white children a basic education in literary and numeracy, and what is increasingly described as 'Christian, English education'. In 1987 the *Sun* newspaper published a story headed 'Odd Boy Out' (*Sun*, 3.5.87) which reported the mother of a white boy at an East London primary school as claiming that 'Asian children get total priority' and 'the last straw was when he came home talking Indian'. Parents at a Manchester primary school formed a 'Parents English Education Rights' (PEER) group after a mother had complained to a local paper that her son could count in Punjabi but not in English (A. M. Weekend, 8.5.87), and the story was taken up in the national press. Despite protests by the Head of Governors about the inaccurate picture presented of the school, no retractions were published. Subsequently the school contacted parents in an effort to discover how many parents were dissatisfied with the education offered; 78 per cent reported satisfaction and some of the white parents who had initially joined PEER dissociated themselves.

The most publicized dispute of the 1980s between white parents and educationalists began in September 1987 when 22 Dewsbury parents refused to send their children to Headfield Church of England school, to which they had been allocated, and where 85 per cent of the pupils were of Asian origin. For a year the parents defied the Kirklees Local Education Authority and took their case to the High Court, supported by Baroness Cox, a long standing opponent of multicultural education (Cox, 1986), and by the Parental Alliance for Choice in Education. The children were educated for a year in a school set up by the parents. The dispute ended in July 1988 when the authority capitulated, and allowed the parents to send their children to Overthorpe, a predominantly white school (Midgley, 1988). The High Court had ruled that the authority had failed to publish clear guidelines on school catchment areas and admission policies. The authority accepted the blame for administrative 'mistakes' and the Director of Education was criticized in a formal report on the affair.

The Dewsbury case gave wide publicity to white parental claims that the Headfield curriculum was unsuitable for white pupils and that standards were lowered by the focus on the needs of the Asian children (Roy and St John Brooks, 1987). In court, the parents' counsel had claimed that 'the parents have a natural desire that their children should be educated in a traditional English and Christian environment' (Naylor 1988a). The Headteacher and Governors of Headfield had always insisted that the curriculum offered was 'English and Christian' and was no different to that of the favoured Overthorpe school. In addition, teachers refuted the suggestion that standards at the school were lowered by the presence of Asian children. Indeed, a 19-year-old Asian former pupil collected evidence that some 30 of his Headfield contemporaries were currently studying at higher degree level. Despite claims that the Headfield incident was not 'racial' the Chief Inspector of police in West Yorkshire reported a 40 per cent increase in racial attacks in Dewsbury which he attributed to the dispute (*Independent*, 2.9.88).

Support for segregation

The Dewsbury dispute had major significance for the possibility of increased racial segregation in urban schools. Although the Dewsbury case was successful on the grounds of administrative errors by the Authority, the 1988 Education Act offers parents greater freedom of choice and the possibility that they can legally refuse to send their children to multi-ethnic schools. A Derbyshire parental association was reported in 1987 as 'watching the Dewsbury situation closely' and claimed that parents and teachers in many areas of the country were dissatisfied with multicultural developments in the curriculum and with accommodating minorities and their religions to the extent that 'being a white, Christian country' was lost (Wilson, 1987). The Derby Professional Association of Teachers was also reported to be in favour of 'declaring that parents who don't want to send their children to a school where the vast majority of pupils are of ethnic minority origin should not be forced to do so' (Wilson, *op. cit.*).

It is, however, difficult to establish whether, given the choice, a majority of white parents would prefer to have their children educated in all-white schools. A Harris poll for London Weekend Television, carried out in November 1987, reported that 40 per cent of white parents in the South East favoured a school 'of their own race' as against 19 per cent of Asian parents and 15 per cent of Afro-Caribbean parents. In the Home Counties over 50 per cent of white parents favoured all-white schools, but in multiracial areas this dropped to 22 per cent (Sutcliffe, 1987). Thus, contrary to well-publicized cases of white hostility at individual multiracial schools, white parents at such schools may be becoming more tolerant of their children being educated alongside minority group children. It is white parents who do not meet minorities in their areas who are more likely to support segregated schools.

The extent of support for parental organization opposing multi-cultural and multi-faith developments is also too difficult to gauge. There is a number of small 'new right' organizations, following the same broad philosophy, claiming wide parental support, and with some individuals active in several of the organizations (Hempel, 1988), whose policies aim to encourage segregation on religious grounds. Naylor, honorary secretary to the Parental Alliance for Choice in Education, and a supporter of the Dewsbury parents, announced in 1988 that the organization would support Muslim parents in their demands for voluntary-aided Muslim schools. 'Members of non-Christian faiths are demanding protection from the multicultural mish-mash served in schools . . . legitimate demands for separate schools and distinctive education are growing' (Naylor, 1988a). In his capacity as a councillor in Salisbury, Wiltshire, Naylor has also opposed the work of the Wiltshire ESG project described in chapter six, castigating multicultural developments both in Kirklees and Wiltshire as 'totalitarian' and run by 'multicultural zealots' (Naylor, 1988b).

There are undoubtedly many white parents who would be pleased to see separate Muslim voluntary-aided schools set up as a way of separating white children from children perceived as both racially and culturally alien, and who would support organizations opposing curriculum changes appropriate for a multicultural society. However, there are also white parents who are now no longer opposed to their children being educated with minority group children and who support a more appropriate 'education for all' which is government policy in the 1980s.

Summary
The Swann Committee argued that failure to acknowledge the predominantly negative racial attitudes of white pupils, and commit the educational system to making appropriate change constitutes a

'fundamental miseducation'. This chapter has presented evidence that in the 1980s white pupils' views of, and attitudes towards, racial and cultural minorities are still predominantly those of the 'white superiority' deplored by *Racial Unity* in the 1950s. The views are fuelled by new antagonisms and misinformation, and occasionally demonstrate a desperate reluctance to abandon hostile beliefs and a need to scapegoat minorities for personal and social disadvantages. The views cannot simply be morally condemned as racist. They illustrate six suggested nationalistic themes, which are all supported and reinforced by the nationalistic views of political leaders, by immigration and nationality legislation, by the media and by the antagonistic views of parents and local communities. The views also reflect the paradoxes and hypocrisy that Dench has suggested characterize other democratic societies.

An overview of evidence of white parental views since the 1960s suggests that the overt antagonisms some white parents felt about the education of their children alongside minority children still persists in some areas in the 1980s. Those parents seeking to have their children educated in predominantly white schools were given wider parental choice by the 1988 Education Act and could count on the support of the 'new right' organizations supporting school segregation. However, there is also some evidence of greater acceptance of multiracial schools by white parents in multiracial areas.

The views of white parents in white areas are not well researched, but evidence indicates that antagonism towards those regarded as racially or culturally different is still the norm, and white parents continue to influence their children to hold negative views of minorities and to condone or ignore racist behaviour.

On the positive side, there is some encouraging evidence from the Swann data, and the north-east schools, that some pupils are thinking in terms of acceptance, sympathy and respect for minorities, and are beginning to concede the unfairness of discriminatory treatment. There is also evidence that there are committed practitioners who are attempting to capitalize on pupils' positive views, and are attempting to develop curriculum and classroom practices that will begin to educate pupils towards a belief in equal citizenship and equal respect for ethnic minorities.

The next chapter examines the strength of imperial beliefs which, incorporated into the curriculum, provide at least part of an explanation for continuing racial antagonisms and the perpetuation of beliefs of white superiority.

Notes

1 An M. Ed. in Multicultural Education was offered on a part-time basis at Sunderland Polytechnic from 1987.

2 This study was undertaken for the MacDonald Committee of Inquiry into the murder of an Asian boy at a Manchester school in 1986 (Kelly and Cohen, 1988).

3 The ESG project worker in Cumbria began to collect evidence of racist behaviour where parents of victims preferred to ignore or minimize the incident to avoid further harassment.

4 The National Association for Multi-racial Education became the National Anti-racist Movement in Education in 1985.

Appendix to Chapter 2

Racial and ethnic name-calling by children

Children under 13	Children over 13
blackie	allah
black bastard	ape
black face	asian
black jack	banana
black lagoon	bindu
black shit	blackie
brownie	black arsehole
bud bud	black bastard
burnt toast	black jack
chinaman	black mammy
coon	blue lagoon
ethiopian	brown sauce
foreigner	chalky
greasy mop	chimpanzee
honky	chink, chinky
hong kong fooler	dago
half-breed	darkie
indian dog	foreigner
irish git	french frog
irish nigger	full moon
italian pizza	gandhi
italian wop	golliwog
jew, jew boy	gorilla
jewish bastard	guinness drinker
kaffir	hindu
kraut	honkey
little white monkey	hot chocolate
mafia boss	immigrant
nigger	jap
nignog	jew, jewbag

paki
paki lover
pepperelli
pizza head
polish
shithead
slave
spade
spaghetti bolognaise
wog
wop

jungle bunny
leprechaun
mick
monkey
munjab
nigger
nignog lover
paddy
paki
paki lover
pizza
poppadum
potato eater
ranjam
ravi shankar
sambo
spanish omelette
spear chucker
spic
spud
turk
whitey
wog
wop
wooden spoon
yank
yid
zulu

Source: Kelly, E. and Cohen, T. (1988), *Racism in Schools, New Research Evidence*, Trentham Books, pp. 58 & 59.

3 The imperial curriculum

> The curriculum appropriate to our imperial past cannot meet the require-
> ments of modern Britain.
>
> (DES, 1977, p. 4)

Chapter six of the Swann Report – the core chapter discussing the
meaning of 'Education for All' – was clear that 'offering all pupils a
good, relevant, and up-to-date education for life in Britain and the
world as it is today' (DES, 1985a, p. 315) would involve considerable
change in a school curriculum which reflected ethnocentric[1] values and
attitudes inappropriate both to the changed nature of British society
and to Britain's place in the world.

The recognition that the curriculum was, and still is, in many ways
influenced by the beliefs and values of a period of imperial enthusiasm
and a final expansion of the British Empire – a period which coincided
with the development of mass education[2] – has however been afforded
little discussion. Yet it was during this period of Empire that many
aspects of what is now regarded as 'British culture' came to be
reflected in the school curriculum, underpinned by a set of values still
regarded by many as 'traditional' British values. Some of these values
were and are highly questionable in terms of democracy, tolerance,
and social and racial justice. They reflected a dominant world-view
which was not 'traditional' at all but was created from the 1880s by
dominant social and political élites and spread, by education and by
imperial propaganda (MacKenzie, 1984, p. 2), into popular consciousness. This world-view was one in which imperialism, a revived
militarism, and unpleasant racial beliefs derived from social
Darwinism fused to create a popular consciousness that the British
'race' had a particular superiority vis-à-vis the rest of the world.
Several historians of British society have dated the period from the
1880s to the 1950s as a time when a 'core ideology' of imperialism
emerged, characterized by values of moral superiority, race
patriotism, and xenophobia (Field, 1982; MacKenzie, 1984). Readers
of popular newspapers in the Britain of the 1980s could hardly doubt

that feelings of moral superiority and offensive views of other nations are still part of 'traditional' British values.

It is this world-view, and these inappropriate values, reflected in parts of the school curriculum, which the Swann Committee characterized as ethnocentric, and which led the Committee to declare a concern with 'bringing about a fundamental reorientation of the attitudes which condition the selection of curriculum materials', to help pupils 'analyse critically and rationally the nature of British society in a global context' (DES, 1985a, p. 324).

However, the myth of English superiority engendered during the period of imperialism and supported by nineteenth-century scientific racism, is still strong, and there is currently much tension between those who believe that there is an unproblematic British heritage – a set of values which should be unquestionably reflected in the school curriculum – and those who consider that it is now time to disentangle the curriculum from the imperial past. For these latter, there is undoubtedly a need to develop a curriculum based on a more apropriate, but as yet not properly defined, set of values.

This chapter examines some influences on the state school curriculum in the late nineteenth and early twentieth centuries, a period when a consciousness of Empire and a popular imperialism was at its height, and a value system was emerging based on a militaristic patriotism and a 'national pride' which by definition excluded non-whites, colonials and foreigners. The influence of public-school values on the developing school curriculum, textbooks which reflected an imperial purpose and patriotic fervour, and juvenile literature which became an early mass medium for disseminating imperial values, are discussed. The aim of this chapter is to begin to probe the strength of imperial values and beliefs, which, by underpinning the school curricula and educational activities, have influenced several generations of white adults in twentieth-century Britain, including parents of children currently in our schools. Many people, including many teachers, are not aware of the extent of the British Empire; a list of territories acquired over 300 years, and dates of autonomy of these territories, is appended to this chapter.

History, values and curriculum

Writing in 1973 Brian Simon noted that the curriculum, the central feature of formal education, is 'virtually a virgin field of historical study' (Simon, 1973, p. 144). The historical research into the values underpinning curriculum development at particular periods, as the persistence of these values, is crucial to understanding current ideas and practices.

Educationalists need to be careful when linking historical and contemporary events. Silver (1977) and others have rightly pointed out the dangers of 'raiding history' to prove contemporary points. However, curriculum theorists have, until relatively recently, been more inclined to neglect an historical dimension in their work, than to raid history, and few have attempted to link the values underlying current curriculum content with the past.

Raymond Williams, one of the most perceptive analysts of cultural values and education, laid the foundations for a study of history, values and the curriculum. In 1965 he wrote that:

> an educational curriculum expresses a compromise between an inherited selection of interests and the emphasis of new interests. At various points in history even this compromise may be long delayed and will often be muddled. The fact about our present curriculum is that it was essentially created by the nineteenth century.
>
> (Williams, 1965, p. 171–2)

His view was that in order to discuss education sensibly, the cultural choices involved in the selection of curriculum content must be examined in historical terms; this would allow an understanding of the influences on choices, and the emphases, ommissions and distortions present within a particular curriculum. Lawton (1975), used Williams's insights to argue that developing a curriclum involves not only crucial cultural choices, but also political choices. Theoretical debate about the reflection of cultural values in a curriculum must question who controls and influences the selection of curriculum knowledge, and which social groups or controlling élites have the power to influence curriculum decisions. Lawton described a curriculum as 'essentially a selection from the culture of a society; certain aspects and ways of life, certain kinds of knowledge, attitudes and values, are regarded as so important that their transmission to the next generation is not left to chance' (Lawton, 1975, p. 6.) but *who* makes the 'selection' is of course of the greatest importance. Because the school curriculum is a transmitter of cultural values, curriculum study must focus on the dominant ideas and values which come to be reflected in schools and question the origins of these values. This means that an historical dimension to contemporary curriculum study is vital.

There is currently some interest in remedying past neglect of the historical dimension, and empirical study and analysis of curriculum from an historical perspective is now being undertaken (Goodson, 1983; Goodson and Ball, 1984.) One analysis of the social, political and economic premises which acted on the curriculum in the nine-teenth and twentieth century has been provided by Gordon and

Lawton (1978). They show how powerful individuals and pressure groups were able to influence the content of the curriculum, the pedagogy and, by implication, the values which lay beneath the selection and transmission of certain kinds of knowledge.

They quote, for example, an early twentieth-century pressure group, the Moral Instruction League, which was influential enough to ensure that its model syllabus for moral teaching was inserted into the 1906 code of regulation for public elementary schools. The League believed that patriotism was a moral value to be inculcated into children. History teaching was to have a moral and patriotic element – 'it should include for the lower classes, the lives of great men and women, and in the higher classes, a knowledge of the growth of the British Empire' (Gordon and Lawton, 1978, p. 103). Supporters of the moral instruction league included Baden-Powell, the founder of the Scout Movement, General Booth of the Salvation Army, Winston Churchill, and the influential writers Conan Doyle and Rudyard Kipling. In keeping with eugenic ideas of the period, the League was concerned that juvenile indiscipline and 'lack of moral fibre' among the young was a serious social danger that in addition constituted a threat to the security of the Empire. All white people, of whatever social class, were expected to set an example of discipline and industry to the inferior peoples of the Empire. The values of this particular pressure group were able to influence directly the elementary school curriculum.

A more systematic understanding of how a curriculum is negotiated over time, which values become accepted and reflected in the curriculum, and whose interests have been, and are being, served by the selection and retention of certain values, is becoming possible through a study of curriculum history. Only through a more complete historical understanding of the origins of values underpinning what is taught in schools, can changes be made which are required to alter the ethnocentric nature of most of the present-day school curriculum in the direction suggested by the Swann Committee.

It is however, equally important to discover who 'lost' in the struggle to influence the curriculum. For example, Annie Besant, Victorian social reformer and women's rights campaigner, was a vocal opponent of both religious teaching and imperialism in the curriculum, but her views were not powerful enough to influence curriculum planners.

Public-school influence

One way in which the values of a dominant social and political élite came to influence mass education in Britain was via the public schools. There is little doubt that the values of the late nineteenth-century public-school curriculum filtered into the developing state elementary and secondary school curriculum of the early twentieth century, and that these values uncompromisingly reflected an ideology of imperialism. Mangan, a historian of Empire, recorded his view that 'the British Empire was run by public schoolboys' and that the curriculum values imbibed by public schoolboys eventually influenced all school pupils (Mangan, 1986, p. 136), although the ideas of imperialism were propagated more slowly in state elementary and grammar schools.

Much imperial propaganda in late nineteenth-century British education was concerned with a growing awareness of empire among public school boys, and the deliberate cultivation of a militaristic imperialism in public schools by Heads and teachers. By the turn of the century a close relationship had developed between the public-school curriculum, service to Empire, and a glorification of imperialism. Lawson-Walton, an exponent of the duties of government to its empire, wrote in the *Contemporary Review* in 1899 that, since the energies of the British race had given them their empire, and as 'British rule . . . of every race brought within its sphere, has the incalculable benefit of just law, tolerant trade, and considerate government' (p. 306) it was the duty of public schools to provide competent rulers and administrators. Many public school headteachers saw this as an important duty, and were willing to educate not only future imperial administrators, but also generals, missionaries, educationists and traders. Mangan (1980, 1986) in his studies of the images of Empire in Victorian and Edwardian public schools, has documented the committed and single-minded imperialism of some headteachers. For example, H. W. Moss, Head of Shrewsbury School from 1872 to 1908, believed fervently that God had entrusted England with the task of creating a Christian Empire to be held together by military means. He set up one of the first public school Cadet Corps – with drill, shooting, camps and reviews by serving officers to lay the foundation of the boys training for their imperial mission. Moss also supported the generally developing militarism of the period, suggesting that public schools should directly train army officers so that 'boys with brains and character would be available for the preservation of English dominions in time of war' (Mangan, 1986, p. 119). J. E. C. Welldon, the Head of Harrow, was another enthusiastic propagandist for Empire. He read a paper to the Royal Colonial Institute in 1895 on 'Imperial Aspects of Education' in which he argued that the public schools must produce the governors, generals and statesmen to run the Empire. 'The boys of today are the statesmen and administrators of tomorrow. In their hands is the future of the British Empire'. Welldon also believed unquestioningly in the moral superiority of white people to govern their 'racial inferiors' and to demand 'instinctive obediance' from non-white imperial subjects, and he was an exponent of the popular view that much imperial strength was derived from the games field – 'In the history of the British Empire it is written that England has owed her sovereignty to her sports' (Welldon quoted in Mangan, 1986, p. 120).

Another head who reflected the values of imperial government, militarism, moral and religious superiority over the imperial subjects, and the healthy discipline acquired on the games field, was H. H. Almond, Headteacher of Loretto School, Edinburgh, from 1862 to 1903. He delivered an annual lecture on 'The Divine Governance of Nations' in which he asserted that God's purpose for the British was to guide world history, and the major purpose of a public school education was to create the 'neo-imperial warrior, untroubled by doubt, firm in conviction, strong in mind and muscle' (Almond quoted in Mangan, 1980, p. 120). Public school headteachers were able to spread their imperial cultural values via their overt and their hidden curricula; sermons, prize day speeches, school magazine editorials all provided means of reinforcing these values, and they were also able, in a boarding school setting, to restrict access to alternative views, and influence an adolescent educational élite to the point where the values were internalized strongly enough to provide a life-long basis for action. Mangan describes the public school values of the time as based on four spheres of social and political consciousness. There was, among the élite groups governing Britain and the Empire a need to establish in their young an ideal of selfless service, a sense of racial superiority, a sense of imperial chauvenism and an uncritical acceptance of the rightness of these views and values (Mangan, 1986, p. 116).

Upper- and upper-middle-class pupils at public schools were encouraged by their headteachers to believe that it was natural that those who ruled the country and the Empire should be selected from their schools. The schools became places where the education embodied the whole tradition and values of the dominant upper classes.

The imperial training required by the upper classes did however, take a very practical turn. It was not possible to run an Empire on a classical education, particularly if trade and exchange of goods were involved. A mathematics textbook, first published in 1874, deplored the fact that 'many persons who are supposed to have received the best education which the country affords, are in matters of numerical information ignorant and helpless, in a manner which places them in this respect far below members of the middle class' (Colenso, 1892, preface).

Arithmatical training for future imperial rulers required them to complete such examination questions as

> *Question 14*: A rupee contains 16 annas and 12 pice : Find, in French money, the annual interest, at 3.5 per cent, on 5217 rup. 3 an. 6 pi. – exchange 2.63 francs per rupee.
>
> (Colenso, 1892, p. 188)

The answer for those slow to calculate is 480 fr. 24.5 cents. For future engineers of the Empire, question 28 from examination paper 15 of this textbook, required boys to work out the following:

> *Question 24*: Of the whole cost of contracting a railway, $^5/_7$ is held in shares, and the remaining £400,000 was borrowed on mortgage at 5%. Find what amount of gross annual receipts, of which 40% will be required for the working expenses of the line, and 8% for a reserve fund, will yield to the shareholders a dividend of 4.5 per cent on their investments.
>
> (Colenso, 1892, p. 206)

Filtering of values

The importance of the values underpinning the public school curriculum was not only that they pervaded the schooling of imperial and later commonwealth administrators, but that these values percolated from the public schools to other schools – the higher elementary schools and the state grammar schools. By the end of the First World War the values of Empire had become part of the consciousness of the state education system. Values which comprised elements of nationalism, militarism, and racial arrogance, combined with beliefs in superior moral and Christian benevolence towards imperial subjects had become incorporated in the school curriculum offered to the majority of the nations children (many of them to grandparents of children at school in the 1980s). Some evidence of this percolation into an elementary school curriculum in early twentieth-century Britain is provided by Roberts's account of a childhood in Salford, *The Classic Slum* (1971). Roberts detailed the way in which the state school teachers copied their public school 'superiors' in fostering an ethnocentric view of imperial greatness, and led the middle and working classes towards a 'staunch patriotism' based extensively on racial superiority. 'The public school ethos, . . . distorted into myth, . . . set standards and ideals . . . for slum boys' (Roberts, 1971, p. 127). The schools provided models for the rest of the education system, and their values become part of the values embedded in state school curricula and extra curricula activities. The work of MacKenzie and others (MacKenzie, 1984, 1986) has strikingly demonstrated the many aspects of juvenile life affected by public-school ideas of Empire.

Certainly by the 1920s, the symbols and rituals of imperial life had become part of the state curriculum – school loyalties were manipulated for imperial ends, magazines and speech days extolled the activities of boys in the Empire and imperial campaigns. Roberts also noted that children welcomed the flag-waving, processions, bands, uniforms and royal visits, as a relief from routine, often accompanied as they were, by free patriotic mugs, buns and chocolate (Roberts, 1971, p. 23), and he drew attention to the almost religious fervour with which teachers 'spelled out patriotism', drawing attention to the massed areas of red on the world maps which 'belonged to us'.

Humphries (1981) in a study of early twentieth-century working-class youth, has noted the way in which belief in racial inferiority and the social inferiority of the working class came together at the period. Images of working class degeneracy were translated into jungle metaphors – 'slum monkey', or 'brute savages', 'aping' undesirable practices, metaphors which are still stock racial insults in classrooms in the 1980s. Those controlling working-class education sought to infuse the values that would serve economic interest and the interests of social order – hard work, discipline and thrift, and also the patriotic militaristic values filtering down from public schools. Humphries refers to 'the imperialist elements in the school curriculum, which, combined with jingoistic juvenile literature, did exercise an important influence on the thought and feelings of some working-class youth' (p. 42). Imperialist values were derived from a curriculum imitation of the public-school ethos and as one of Humphries's elderly respondents told him 'you could tell by the way they did call them – Froggie, Eyties and Dagoes the only way we'd all describe them was that they were beneath you'. (p. 43).

However, the ideology of imperialism made a direct appeal to some of the values of working-class boys, as it reflected a number of existing cultural 'traditions' – for example, fighting, gang warfare over street territory, and assertions of masculinity. Fighting, racism and sexism were certainly still part of the 'traditional values' exposed by the working-class boys studied by Willis (1977) later in the century.

But the major importance of the cultural values and influences disseminated from the upper to the lower classes, via education, was that the 'lower classes' were encouraged to believe in their economic, political, social and racial superiority to the rest of the empire: 'the domestic underclass could become the imperial overclass' (MacKenzie, 1984, p. 254) and all classes could unite in a comforting national, patriotic solidarity. The strength of this solidarity is demonstrably still present in the late twentieth century, and goes some way towards explaining the xenophobia and racism which are still part of the 'British heritage'.

School textbooks

Ideological justification for imperial expansion, colonial wars and conquest, and the continued subjugation of those whom Rudyard Kipling so eloquently described as 'lesser breeds without the law' was reproduced on a large scale in late Victorian and early Edwardian textbooks and juvenile literature. Many of these texts were reprinted and continued to be used in schools into the 1950s. An example of such a text is Seeley's *The Expansion of Empire* (first published 1883) which set out a simplistic and persuasive account of the benefits of the British Empire to both British subjects at home and overseas, but especially at home. He glossed over the military conquest and exploitation required to obtain such an Empire and became best known for his quotation that 'we have conquered half the world in a fit of absence of mind' (p. 10).

There have been few historical studies of school textbooks and imperial values (but see Chancellor, 1970; Bratton, 1981; MacKenzie, 1984). Those who are currently concerned with an examination of racism in children's literature and school textbooks, and in the production of anti-racist literature, have not yet made systematic attempts to link the values underlying the texts which influenced the grandparents and parents of present-day pupils, and relate these to the values implicit in current texts (but see Klein, 1985). Nor has there been much debate about the policies required to deal with those textbooks and works of literature which encapsulate ideas and values accepted by schools until the 1950s as normal, but which are now widely regarded as inappropriate. The *ad hoc* policies of some LEAs, schools and individuals, in dealing with racist textbooks and fiction (particularly by the removal of such material from libraries) has led to accusations of censorship and has provided an easy political target. The policy of removing some racist textbooks from schools may be necessary but, as one historian of the British Empire has noted, 'moral revulsion may not be the best way to understand the path of Empire' (Lloyd, 1984, p. ix) and there may be ways of using the textbooks of empire to demonstrate how certain values came to be incorporated in the texts, what they demonstrated about the 'British heritage' and why they are no longer appropriate.

One task of the study of school textbooks and educational materials must also be to discover the process by which historically specific values are transferred into particular texts and perpetuated in them as 'facts' or 'right answers'; to do this it is necessary to study the pedagogy of the historical period. Curriculum content, if simplified and taught didactically, can quickly become unalterable and accepted as truth. Reflections of imperialism in educational materials came at a time when new pedagogic techniques were developing in state schools, and new methods of instruction were being urged on teachers via a powerful school inspectorate and teachers manuals. One 'new' method thought particularly useful in the early twentieth century, for teaching working-class pupils, was the simplification of concepts – particularly those used in history and geography – so that 'children would not be harrassed by complicated issues' (Board of Education, 1927). This early promulgation of what would now be regarded as 'low expectations' had the effect of injecting an uncritical approach to textbooks in both teachers and pupils.

The teaching of history and geography, and the reflection of imperial values in the textbooks used, provided a major influence on pupils in the early twentieth century which many teachers still find difficult to question. Inglis, an uncompromising critic of current curriculum values, has pointed out that 'thousands of teachers at all levels . . . believe that many of the commonly accepted answers to old questions are incredible falsehoods', and in particular 'the history we told ourselves for half a century will not do, and was always disgusting' (Inglis, 1985, p. 108). Whether labelled as incredible falsehood or ideology, there is no doubt that late Victorian and Edwardian imperial values became strongly reflected in school textbooks and the values have proved extremely resistent to change.

History, first introduced into the public school curriculum by Arnold at Rugby, was gradually introduced into state schools but did not become compulsory in senior elementary and secondary schools until 1900. Geography was more popular, being taught in most elementary and secondary schools from the 1890s, which was a period of increased publication of both history and geography textbooks. This was also the period when 'a single ideological slant was introduced into all school texts' McKenzie (1984, p. 177). This 'slant' was a convergence of ideas of patriotism, militarism, respect for monarchy, support for imperial expansion and dominance, and racial superiority. In the textbooks, the past was skewed to fit the current ideas. For example, issues such as the American Civil War, and slavery, were glossed over, moral responsibility for conflict was shifted to colonial countries, ommissions and half-truths encouraged pupils to believe that the territorial and commercial wars fought to acquire the Empire were unavoidable but led ultimately to benefits for the conquered, colonized countries.

A popular history textbook issued by the Board of Education in 1902 (Finnemore, 1902) suggested that lessons on 'Great Englishmen' was a suitable method of teaching history to higher elementary classes. In this text the presentation of the 'natives' who fought to resist imperial rule as possessed by evil ill-feeling towards benevolent and just rulers, was a persistent theme, and their cruelty during rebellions, particularly to English women and children living in the colonies, was stressed. Clive of India 'made the English supreme over that vast country' (Finnemore, p. 188), and Sir Henry Havelock and Lord Roberts suppressed the India mutiny in which 'English women and children were called upon to suffer horrors and tortures to which one cannot give a name' (p. 237). The emotive language of this book – the 'pluck, endurance and heroic bravery' (p. 255) of the British troops, always contrasted with the 'fiends incarnate' who were resisting imperial rule – was part of the hidden curriculum intended to instill attitudes in school pupils towards imperial subjects overseas.

The supposed beneficial effects of British rule was also a constant theme in both history and geography textbooks, which has continued to be reflected in textbooks used relatively recently. One geography textbook, used in Britain until the 1960s, stressed the beneficial and civilizing influence of Britain's role in helping Africa to modernize:

> Under the guidance of Europeans, Africa is steadily being opened up, . . . doctors and scientists are working to improve the health of the Africans, missionaries and teachers are educating the people, . . . the single fact remains that the Europeans have brought civilisation to the peoples of Africa, whose standard of living has, in most cases, been raised by their contact with white people.
>
> (Stembridge, 1956, p. 347.)

This paternalistic view in which the Empire was presented as devoted to the civilization and well-being of subordinate races, was certainly promulgated in many history and geography textbooks until changes in approach, content and method in these subjects developed in the 1960s. The sense of racial and cultural superiority generated by the values implicit in these textbooks was passed on to a receptive white majority in Britain.

Juvenile literature

It was not only in textbooks that images of moral, racial, political and technological superiority of the white races appeared. From the 1880s an expansion of popular publishing, and the creation of a wider readership came at the same time as the development of mass education and wider literacy. One publishing market which proved popular until well after the Second World War, was that of juvenile literature –children's journals, magazines and later, comics.[3] From the 1880s, much of this literature took the form of an adventure tradition 'replete with militarism and patriotism, in which violence and high spirits became legitimized as part of the moral force of a superior race'

(MacKenzie, 1984, p. 199). The adventure literature influenced present-day writers and government officials. For example, the imperial romances of Rider Haggard, which were imbued with racist ideas, influenced the novelist Graham Greene, who is still writing in the 1980s.

The adventure literature was mainly designed for boys, and many of the fictional tales were set in public schools which provided another avenue by which public school imperial values could influence state school pupils. Roberts, wrote of the way in which he and his friends in back-street Salford became 'avid for the fictional world of the [public] school' (1971, p. 127) and noted particularly the influence of 'Greyfriars', the public school invented by Frank Richards as a setting for serialized stories in the popular journals *Magnet* and *Gem*. The public schoolboy hero became an influential figure with whom several generations of state schoolboys identified. Rudyard Kipling's *Stalky and Co.* (1899) which extolled the high spirits, patriotic pride and intrepid self-reliance of a group of public schoolboys destined to be military leaders of Empire, was serialized on British television in the 1980s.

An increasing number of boys' adventure journals were produced from 1880, which presented an imperial world-view suffused with nationalistic, militaristic and racial ideas, incorporated into adventure stories which also appealed to romantic emotions. Bratton has noted that in many journals 'an overwhelming surface impression is that of a blatant reiteration of racial pride, militaristic values and a coarse enthusiasm for conflict' (1986, p. 77). Intellect was not prized, physical powers and action were important, and in some stories:

> the world becomes a vast adventure playground in which anglo-saxon superiority can be repeatedly demonstrated vis-à-vis all other races, most of whom are depicted as treacherous and evil.
>
> (MacKenzie, 1984, p. 204)

Roberts (1971) has written that the public school ethos distorted into myth and 'sold weekly in penny numbers' did set standards and ideals, and imperialistic arrogance *became* a 'value' to be accepted.

The Tarzan stories, written by Edgar Rice Burroughs, are probably one example of this view of the world. These stories have had a powerful impact throughout the century, being continually presented on film, and later on television, and serialized extensively in magazines and comic strips. In the stories, Tarzan's breeding, and aristocratic European background, which enabled him to become an educated gentleman in the 'jungle' are continually stressed against the 'treacherous savage natives' he is constantly fighting. His breeding apparently allowed him to kill black people with deliberate cruelty. In *Tarzan the Untamed* (Burroughs, 1919) Tarzan could not 'resist the pleasures of black-baiting, an amusement and a sport in which he had grown even more proficient'. In this story 'black-baiting' included torturing fellow-humans before killing them.

Other stories however, stressed the romance of Empire, and many school textbooks as well as juvenile fiction included the word 'romance' in their title. For example, T. C. Jacks's *Romance of Empire* series and the Seeley Service *Library of Romance* included such titles as *The Romance of Modern Pathfinders*, *The Romance of Savage Life* and *The Romance of Missionary Heroism*. In all the literature, the personal bravery of heroic individuals was a constant theme, which was also extended to include an individual identity for England. In naval adventure stories in particular, 'England is a gallant little nation whose power and conquests are obviously the reward of merit, since all her opponents are bigger and uglier than she is . . . the officers were wonderfully good at inspiring their men, and able to carry out audacious manoeuvres under the noses of lumbering of befuddled foreigners' (Bratton, 1986, pp. 83–4). There are parallels here with the values implicit in the propaganda produced during the Falklands War in 1982.

Of all the imperialistic boys' adventure magazines produced in the 1880s, *Union Jack* was perhaps more influential than most. Its second editor, G. A. Henty, wrote over 80 boys' adventure stories himself, and employed well-known writers of the period to write for the magazine, including Conan Doyle, Jules Verne and Robert Stevenson. Henty, like other boys' writers in the late nineteenth and early twentieth centuries, had personal experience of colonial warfare and war reporting. He also had strong racial and militaristic views, and his schoolboy heroes exhibited both class snobbery and racial prejudice. Their superior morality was associated with their public school education and their Nordic complexions; many of Henty's stories were both anti-black, and anti-semitic. Non-whites were presented as unfit to govern themselves, and the energy and self-reliance of Northern Europeans was contrasted with the lethargy, fatalism and ignorance of non-whites. To be white and British provided a moral and ethical base-line for judging all other nations, and races, who were always found wanting. *Union Jack* ceased publication in 1933, *Magnet* and *Gem* during the Second World War, but other publications came to replace these, particularly the comics *Rover* (1922), *Wizard* (1922), *Skipper* (1930) and *Hotspur* (1933) in which an imperial world view and notions of national and racial superiority, continued to be presented.

Long after contemporary realities and intellectual thought had moved on, the same complacent self-confidence, sense of national and racial superiority, and suspicious xenophobia continued to be the principle characteristics of children's literature.

(MacKenzie, 1984, p. 224)

Summary

This chapter has attempted to demonstrate that the development of mass education, and the filtering of ideas and values from public to state schools, coincided with the height of a popular imperialism, which was particularly reflected in school textbooks and juvenile literature. The intensity of ethnocentric beliefs in the glories of Empire, white superiority, and a militaristic 'patriotism', were uncritically reflected in textbooks and other literature; and were reinforced by pedagogic techniques which encouraged simplification of complex moral issues, and unthinking acceptance of value-laden curriculum content.

The importance of these imperial values and beliefs is two-fold. Not only are they still reflected, although in changed or rationalized ways, in much current curriculum material, thus influencing the present generation of school children, they have undoubtedly influenced the grandparents and parents of children currently in schools. The task of changing the curriculum has to take account of the past influences which now form part of the 'British heritage'. Some attempts at curriculum change, and resistance to such attempts, are the subject of the next chapter.

Notes

1   To be ethnocentric means to view the World totally from one point of view, to some extent all education systems are ethnocentric.

2   The period 1870–1920 is taken in this chapter as the time when mass education developed, and an ideology of imperialism was at its height.

3   J. S. Bratton has pointed out (in MacKenzie, 1986) that to attempt to quantify the presence of imperialism in the thousands of juvenile publications of the Victorian and Edwardian periods would be impossible, but selections from the literature can demonstrate the way in which fiction encapsulated and transmitted imperial values.

Appendix to Chapter 3

Territories of the British Empire

Name of state or colony	Date of acquisition	Date of autonomy and/or leaving the Commonwealth
Aden (South Yemen)	1839	1967
Anguilla	1650	–
Antigua	1632	–
Australia (various territories)	1788–1859	1852–1890
Bahamas	1629	1973
Bangla Desh (East Pakistan)	1757–1842	1947
Barbados	1625	1966
Belize (British Honduras)	1638–1802	1982
Bermuda	1609	–
Botswana (Bechuanaland)	1884	1966
British Antarctica	1819–1832	–
British Indian Ocean Territories	1815	1960
British Somaliland	1884 –1887	1960
British Virgin Islands	1672	–
Brunei	1888	1983
Burma	1826 –1885	1948
Canada (various territories)	1670–1849	1847–1871
Cayman Islands	1670	–
Cyprus	1878	1960
Dominica	1763	1978
Egypt	1882–1914	1922
Falkland Islands	1833	–
Fiji	1874	1970
Florida	1763	1783
Gambia	1661–1713	1965
Ghana (Gold Coast)	1821–1901	1957
Gibraltar	1704–1713	–
Grenada	1763	1974
Guyana (British Guiana)	1796 –1815	1966
Heligoland	1807–1814	1890
Hong Kong	1842	(Due for secession 1997)
India	1757–1842	1947
Ionian Islands	1815	1864
Iraq	1948–1923	1932
Ireland (Irish Free State)	1169–1606	1921–1949
Jamaica	1655–1670	1962
Kenya	1887–1895	1963
Kiribati (Gilbert Islands)	1892–1918	1979
Lesotho (Bsutoland)	1868	1966
Malawi (Nyasaland)	1889–1891	1904

Malaysia	1786 –1882	1957–1963
Malta	1800–1814	1964
Mauritius	1815	1968
Minorca	1708–1713	1782–1783
Montserrat	1632	
Nauru	1919	1968
New Zealand	1840	1852
Nigeria	1861–1903	1960
Pakistan (separated from India)	–	1947–1972
Palestine (Israel)	1917–1923	1948
Papua New Guinea	1884 –1919	1975
Pitcairn Islands	1838–1887	–
St Christopher Nevis	1624–1628	1983
St Helena, Ascension, Tristan da Cunha	1661–1816	–
St Lucia	1814	1979
St Vincent and Grenadines	1627	1979
Seychelles	1814	1976
Singapore	1819–1824	1963–1965
Solomon Isles	1893–1900	1978
South Africa (various states)	1795–1902	1872–1910
South West Africa (Namibia)	1915–1919	1960
Sri Lanka (Ceylon)	1815	1948
Sudan	1898	1954
Surinam (Dutch Guiana)	1651	1668
Swaziland	1890–1902	1968
Tanzania (Tanganyika and Zanzibar)	1870–1919	1961–1964
(Thirteen Colonies) USA	1636–1732	1776
Tonga	1900	1970
Transjordan (Jordan)	1917–1923	1946
Trinadad and Tobago	1802–1815	1962
Turks and Caicos Islands	1638	–
Tuvalu (Ellice Isles)	1892–1918	1978
Uganda	1888–1895	1962
United Kingdom (England, Wales, Scotland, Ireland)	1707–1801	–
Vanatu (New Hebrides)	1887–1906	1980
Western Samoa	1919	1901–1970
Zambia (Northern Rhodesia)	1889–1900	1964
Zimbabwe (Southern Rhodesia)	1888–1893	1980

Source: Adapted from Lloyd, T. O., *The British Empire 1558–1983*, Oxford University Press, pp. 405–411.

4 The multicultural curriculum

There can be no real argument for a multicultural curriculum. To adopt such a curriculum is to fail to transmit either the common culture of Britain, or the high culture that has grown from it.

(Scruton, 1986, p. 134)

The conventional curriculum is still a vehicle for racism.

(Gill, 1987, BBC TV)

Moves to disentangle the curriculum from the imperial past began to be made in multiracial schools from the early 1970s. Practitioners in those schools observed that the absence of curriculum policies which took account of the presence of minorities led to the perpetuation of stereotypes, prejudices and misinformation, and the populist view that the presence, cultures and life-styles of minority pupils constituted a problem, reinforced a dominant, mono-cultural curriculum approach. By the later 1970s there was considerable agreement among educationalists that the curriculum needed changing to reflect the multiracial, multicultural society, and Britain's changing post-imperial position in the world. There was also some agreement that curriculum change was needed in all schools, not just in multiracial schools. During the 1980s official policy endorsed the development of a curriculum for what official documentation described as an 'ethnically diverse society'. More teachers began to write about their changed practices and serious attempts were made to define what a curriculum based on multicultural and non-racist approaches would look like. The notion of curriculum permeation became popular – practitioners, writers of text-books, and publishers thinking more carefully about the incorporation of multicultural and global approaches in science, mathematics, language and literature, the arts, history, geography and social studies, home economics, religious education and other curriculum areas. By the mid 1980s, encouraged by the Swann Committee's commitment to a more appropriate 'Education For All', the majority of Local Education Authorities were committed to 'changing teaching and curricula to reflect the pluralist nature of society' in all schools (Craft, 1986, p. 83).

However, multicultural curriculum reformers have faced a daunting task. There has been little popular or political support for teaching all pupils something about the background, cultures and life-experiences of former colonial settlers and their children, and even less for helping white pupils to examine their own attitudes towards minorities. Neither has there been much enthusiasm for re-examining the relationship of Britain to her former Empire, or for re-assessing Britain's place in relation to the rest of the world. There has been instead a growing and determined attack on any such changes in curriculum content or approaches by those educational nationalists who represent multicultural education as subversive of British culture, likely to be associated with left-wing egalitarianism, leading to lowered standards, and having no support from majority or minority parents. This chapter briefly reviews the consolidating opposition to the kind of curriculum change envisaged by both the Swann Committee and the Secretary of State's instructions to the National Curriculum Council,[1] describes some of the literature produced by subject specialists who have incorporated changes in their subjects, and considers the possibility for further development via the National Curriculum.

Multicultural curriculum aims

Questions about 'what to teach to whom' have underpinned the general and extensive debates on curriculum which have characterized education in the 1980s in Britain. The document *Better Schools* (DES, 1985b) encapsulated a general view that although schools had been expected to expand the range of their tasks to cope with a changing society, there was little clarity or agreement about what were to be the major aims of education. The document listed six 'purposes of learning' and four principles, and specified certain subjects that all pupils should study. In 1988 a subject-specific national curriculum was enshrined in legislation. All pupils aged from 5 to 16 in maintained schools were, from September 1989, to be taught a curriculum consisting of three core and seven foundation subjects, plus religious education and a daily act of worship which was to be of a 'broadly Christian character' (Education Act 1988, Section 7.1). All pupils in maintained schools, whatever their ethnic origin, were to be taught the same curriculum, which accorded with the view of the Parliamentary Home Affairs Committee in 1981 that 'it cannot be over-emphasised that in most respects the curriculum needs of ethnic minority pupils are exactly the same as those of all pupils' (Home Affairs Committee, 1981, p. lxvi). This view, however, left open the question of what the curriculum needs of all pupils in an ethnically diverse society actually are, what the aims of education in such a society should be and how these aims should be translated into 'subject' content.

There has been no shortage of prescriptions on what the aims of a multicultural curriculum *should* be. The most quoted aims were produced by Jeffcoate in 1976 (see Appendix 1 to this chapter) and reprinted in James and Jeffcoate (1981). The Swann Committee drew on Jeffcoate's work, on DES papers, on Schools Council work, on the paper produced by a multicultural working group of the Council for National Academic Awards, and on the views of the Assistant Masters and Mistresses Association, to articulate the broad aims of a good education for all pupils (DES, 1985a, pp. 318–19). The Committee took the view that the aims of multicultural education were synonymous with a good education which aimed to produce decent, just, humane citizens, and they stressed that aims translated into practice not only by changing curriculum content but by changing the attitudes and values which underlie the education process.

> We are not primarily concerned with changing the content of the curriculum, but rather with bringing about a fundamental re-orientation of the attitudes which condition the selection of curriculum materials and subject matter, and which underlie the actual teaching and learning process.
>
> (*op. cit.*, p. 324)

Theoretical elaboration and justification for a multicultural curriculum has been provided world-wide by liberal educationalists (see Lynch, 1983; Banks and Lynch, 1986); a review of literature describing and criticizing multicultural curricula up to 1982 was produced by Tomlinson (1983) and there is extensive literature in Britain on both multicultural and anti-racist curricula. An antagonistic debate which argued that multicultural aims and anti-racist aims were alternatives rather than concomitants – both necessary approaches in an attempt to alter attitudes of white superiority – has been summarized in Troyna (1987) and Carrington and Short (1989). This debate set up what Leicester (1986) described as a 'false dichotomy' and diverted attention from right-wing political critiques. There has been little evidence produced by committed anti-racists to support their contention that those teachers putting into practice multicultural aims were not also challenging the racist beliefs of their pupils. Descriptions of anti-racist teaching, for example Brandt (1987), do not differ greatly from descriptions of teaching labelled as 'merely' multicultural.

One consequence of the multicultural versus anti-racist debate is that it has diverted the attention of, and sometimes antagonized, many of those practitioners wishing to make appropriate curriculum changes. By the later 1980s, protagonists were not facing up to realities. Hatcher, for example, was asserting in 1987 that 'the central debate within multicultural education is between . . . left anti-racists . . . and the new multiculturalism' (Hatcher, 1987, p. 184). By this time in Britain, the central debate was between those who supported any kind of multicultural, non-racist change and the opponents of *any* sort of change in a multicultural direction, who were successfully marginalizing or vilifying the whole issue.

Opposition to a multicultural curriculum

Opposition to any multicultural or anti-racist development was relatively muted from the political and educational right until the 1980s. In the 1970s curriculum change had largely been confined to urban multiracial schools, was associated with the demands of ethnic minority parents, and had produced divisions among supporters. Such developments were regarded as relatively unimportant and unthreatening to the education system as a whole. Once it became apparent that change in all schools for all pupils was advocated and that white areas would be affected, opposition became more vocal. The politicians, academics and educationalists collectively described in chapter one as educational nationalists either formed new pressure groups or re-directed the attention of existing groups such as the Hillgate Group and the Salisbury Group, published literature arguing against any form of multicultural and anti-racist education, influenced parliamentary legislation, and received considerable sympathetic press coverage. Although opposition claimed to be educational, attempting to demonstrate that a multicultural curriculum affected educational standards and was being advocated instead of basic subjects, it was in the main political. The opposition came to centre on the criticisms that multicultural education was associated with, at best, left-of-centre egalitarianism and, at worst, hard-left political subversion, and also that multicultural anti-racist education posed a threat to traditional British values, culture and heritage. Changes in a multicultural direction were especially presented as a threat to Conservative party political values dominant in Britain in the 1980s. At the 1987 Conservative Party conference, the Prime Minister, introducing some of the reforms embodied in the 1988 Education Act, specifically linked left-wing extremism and lowered standards, to supposed anti-racist curriculum developments.

> In the inner cities where youngsters must have a decent education if they are to have a better future, that opportunity is all too often snatched from them by hard-left education authorities and extremist teachers. Children who need to be able to count and multiply are learning anti-racist mathematics, whatever that may be.
>
> (Hughill, 1987)

Political critiques of multicultural, anti-racist education have been closely linked to any kind of educational activity perceived as likely to challenge existing political value-systems, with the assertion that any such challenges were political indoctrination. Thus Cox, in a chapter which criticized the content of an Inner London Education Authority teaching pack on *Auschwitz* (Cox, 1986), claimed that this material 'and many other teaching materials, text books, videos, resource packs in areas ranging from traditional subjects like history and geography to newcomers like World Studies, Peace Studies or Anti-Racist Maths' sets out to indoctrinate pupils and to 'create and foster disaffection, social tension and inter-group conflict' (pp. 79–80). The Hillgate and Salisbury Group publications have also inveighed against world studies, peace studies, sociology, political education, life skills, social awareness courses and 'alien multiculturalism' as providing a framework for propaganda and indoctrination, and for social engineering designed to encourage egalitarianism (see Hillgate Group, 1986, 1987; Scruton, Ellis-Jones and O'Keefe, 1985). The chapters in a book published in 1986 (Palmer, 1986a) brought together a variety of conservative political critiques of multicultural, anti-racist education. The criticisms directed at the Swann Report (DES, 1985a) suggested that while curriculum change advocated by labour-controlled education authorities was likely to be dismissed as indoctrination or subversion, a Department of Education report from a committee chaired by a liberal lord, was regarded as more threatening. Thus Pearce, a member of the right-wing Monday Club, described the report as 'a profoundly dangerous document aimed at the re-shaping of British society' which argued for a 'fundamental change in a national culture regardless of national opinion' (Pearce, 1986, p. 136). Pearce presented the Swann suggestion that a democratic plural society might require a re-thinking of national identity as 'a loss of identity for the native British' who 'have a right to preserve their way of life and this means that it is their culture which must predominate in our schools' (p. 141).

With much of the opposition to a multicultural curriculum centring around a defence of a conservative understanding of the British past, it was not surprising that history teaching became a major area of contention for those opposing a multicultural curriculum. Their British past was expressed in terms of a British heritage and culture being under attack from cultural relativism (Scruton, 1986), from mendacious distortion of history (Palmer, 1986a), or from alternative views of Britain's relationship to Empire, colonies and the Third World. Extensive debates on the role of history in the curriculum, bias in historical content and definitions of historical knowledge and skills took place during the 1980s (see DES, 1985c); Historical Association, (1987) and the inclusion of the skill of 'empathy' in the GCSE syllabus, drew sharp opposition from educational nationalists. Skidelsky (1988) argued that GCSE history was both social engineering and indoctrination, and much of the criticism of the 'new' history centred on its commitment to world history rather than a British-centred history (St John-Brooks, 1988). The *Salisbury Review* stated the Conservative position unequivocally as supporting the teaching of national history 'to restore the lost dimension of British experience, . . . and re-inforce the loyalty on which our survival depends' (Editorial, *Salisbury Review*, 1987).

Versions of history which presented slavery and colonialism from the point of view of the slaves and colonized, have been particularly criticized. Hastie, a former warden of an Inner London History and Social Science Teachers' Centre, censured what he described as 'the race industry's' presentation of past and recent history, as stirring 'needless resentment in the minds of black readers', (Hastie, 1986, p. 73), and Partington, a regular contributor to the *Salisbury Review*, wrote in a police journal in 1982 that 'it is utterly wicked that one-sided and unbalanced diatribes against our colonial past should be unmixed by any consideration of British achievement' (see Gordon and Klug, 1986, p. 33).

A major source of organized opposition to the multicultural curriculum came, in the 1980s, from the variety of small 'new-right' organizations noted in chapter two, which were either parental organizations or claimed wide parental support. These have been documented by Hempel (1988) who noted the overlap of personnel between the groups, and the political influence of some of the members. Thus, the Parental Alliance for Choice in Education, which supported the Dewsbury parents (see chapter two), included on its Council, Professor Sig Prais, who was appointed by the Secretary of State for Education as a Member of the Mathematics Working Group which helped to produce government proposals for the mathematics national curriculum. Not surprisingly, as the section below documents, Professor Prais's group was against the inclusion of any multicultural mathematics. A group calling itself the Campaign for Real Education was set up in 1987 claiming that there had been an 'erosion of the traditional curriculum which emphasised literacy, numeracy and respect and appreciation of our history and culture' by left-wing dominated councils, and that children were being 'abused' by the use of education to change economic, cultural and political values in society (Campaign for Real Education, 1987). Professor Skidelsky, who had campaigned against the new history embodied in the GCSE syllabus, supported this group, and Hempel reported that both the Parental Alliance and the Campaign for Real Education met regularly at the House of Lords, the meetings being chaired by Baroness Cox[2] (Hempel, 1988, p. 16).

Opponents of a multicultural curriculum have claimed that the kind of changes envisaged by the Swann Committee have no parental support and that there has been no parental consultation over the issues (see Honeyford, 1988, pp. 89–93), although Honeyford himself pointed out that parental consultation has never been part of the 'culture of the state educational establishment' (*op. cit.*, p. 92). There is, for example, no record that parents were consulted as to whether teaching 'patriotism' should be including in the elementary school curriculum in the early 1900s (see chapter three). There is certainly evidence that neither majority nor minority parents desire any curriculum activity to be offered as an alternative to the acquisition of educational credentials, or as a low-status curriculum development; any presentation of a multicultural curriculum in these terms has little support. There is evidence, however, that minority parents do wish white pupils to learn to respect and to treat minority pupils as equals, and for all pupils to learn something of the history and cultures of origin of minorities in Britain, 'black' contributions to civilization, reasons for a minority presence and life-styles in Britain, and a broader understanding of world history and of present-day developments in former colonies (see Da Costa, 1988).

Overall, opposition to multicultural and anti-racist curriculum developments slowly became, during the 1980s, a recognizable right-wing political tool for encouraging a populist view that any such developments threatened traditional education. With this kind of opposition it was not surprising that curriculum reformers have found difficulty in persuading colleagues, councillors, parents and others that multicultural and anti-racist aims and activities were in fact directed towards the creation of a more just, decent and humane education system.

Subject development

Opponents of a multicultural curriculum have claimed its activities exist as 'subjects' (Seaton, 1988) or as a 'mish-mash of cultures' (Naylor, 1988a). In reality, multicultural aims and approaches have been directed towards affecting existing school 'subjects' and curriculum activities. Brown (1988b) pointed out that visitors to schools would not find the 'subject' of multiculturalism time-tabled. Instead, they might find 'a variety of classrooms in mainly-white as well as multiracial areas where teachers work hard to help their pupils develop the intellectual skills and emotional maturity within such curriculum areas as humanities, science and languages, to recognise that there are many interpretations of the world . . . and *all* children need to open-mindedly examine them' (p. 41).

During the 1980s, practitioners who wished to add to the content of their subjects, re-direct their subject approaches, alter their teaching methods and question the values underlying their teaching, have been able to turn to a growing literature on subject development. This literature, while stressing the problems inherent in multicultural development, provided useful direction for change and the ESG projects, reported in the following chapters, were able to build on and develop existing ideas. An examination of the development of multicultural and anti-racist approaches within school subjects and activities over the past 20 years would require a separate book, as there is now a very large literature (see Craft and Klein, 1986). The following section describes, briefly, some of the ideas and approaches documented by practitioners in what are now the three core subjects of the school curriculum: Mathematics, Science and English; and in History, one of the foundation subjects.

Mathematics

One of the most sophisticated contributions towards developing multicultural mathematics was provided by Hemming (1984). He pointed out that the universality of mathematics made it an obvious contributor towards a multicultural curriculum and that cultural differences could both enrich the quality of mathematics experience and reduce ideas of cultural superiority. He noted, as an example, the structure of counting systems and the value of learning about a variety of such systems. He also noted the historical debt to Eastern cultures for systems of representation, the Arabic derivation of algebra (*al-jabr*) and the spatial and geometric imagery which forms a basis for mathematical understanding in all cultures. McGowan (1981) has described materials and subject content useful in all classroom, for example, learning the logic behind Chinese chequers, statistical probability from Asian games of chance, and the cultural origin of the 'imperial measure', and Dyson (1986) has explained the ways in which the whole mathematics department in one school incorporated multicultural approaches into schemes of work, and into mathematics cross-curricular approaches relating to Geography, Art and Languages.

Science

Initially, science teachers appeared to find it difficult to accept that multicultural changes were relevant to their subjects, taking the view that their work was universal, neutral and objective. However, by the late 1970s some text-books were beginning to take account of historical and cross-cultural dimensions. Atherton and Lawrence, in *Chemistry for Today and Tomorrow* (1978), illustrated the world-wide develop-ment of chemistry, particularly stressing African contributions, and Haber, in *Black Pioneers of Science and Invention* (1978) demon-strated how the contributions of black scientists had often been ignored. Richmond (1981) wrote perceptively on the qualities neces-sary for a good scientist – curiosity, compassion and competence demanding an understanding of fellow human beings and a desire to work as equals. He noted that science particularly requires a facility for shared communication which can only come from cross-national respect and understanding. Wyn-Williams (1984) documented a history of chemistry and showed how world-wide contributions belie the idea that it is a white, European invention. Biology teachers also began to document the value of their subject in establishing a framework where open enquiry and discussion could dispel racist images and stereotypes which have frequently been presented as having scientific justification. Vance (1984), a black biology teacher, wrote that he became acutely aware of Eurocentric images of Third World countries as 'rife with disease and needing the science of the West to combat their problems' (p. 148). He also noted the way in which nationalist propaganda under the guise of 'science' asserted that races were different and that racism was natural, not bigotry. Watts (1986) also drew attention to the way in which much science teaching perpetuated the idea of the white, male, European or North American scientist as the most important contributors to science (also a view that the ESG workers in Croydon, reported in chapter six of this book, found perpetuated) and she stressed the role that science can play in challenging racial and cultural stereotypes.

English

English, as Craft and Klein (1986) pointed out, has lent itself well to education for a multicultural, non-racist society, and English teachers have pioneered, documented and evaluated successful multicultural innovations in the areas of literature, language and media studies, and have also pioneered linked approaches in drama and dance. The National Association for the Teaching of English, the Centre for Information on Language Teaching and Research (CILT), the Inner London Education Authority's English Centre, and other organiza-tions, have all promoted multicultural approaches in literature and language teaching. English teachers have also been involved in the antagonistic debates which developed over whether and how to

remove out-dated and racially derogatory literature and textbooks
from school libraries and classrooms. English teachers in multiracial
classrooms in the 1970s saw a need to broaden the range of literature in
classrooms and by the 1980s, English teachers in all schools were
probably the largest group of subject specialists developing multicultural curriculum approaches. They have worked closely with
teachers of English as a Second Language, have been involved in
debates demonstrating bilingualism as an educational resource rather
than a liability and, from the time of the report of Lord Bullock's
committee on *Language Across The Curriculum* (1975), have been
concerned to take a broad approach to language and its development
in cross-curricular themes. Bleach (1984) noted that by the 1980s
English teachers had come to read more widely in linguistics, cultural
and historical fields; studying and teaching literature produced by
writers with colonial pasts, and literature from Asia, African and the
Caribbean. She also documented the way in which community writing
by both young and established members of minority groups in Britain
has become an important source of multicultural texts, suggested ways
in which all pupils could learn to compare multi-ethnic with monocultural texts, and pointed to the rapid growth both in the USA and
Britain of literature and juvenile fiction which documents intercultural
tensions and resolutions in a modern rather than an imperialistic
manner. Craft and Klein (1986, p. 46) have pointed out that support
for bilingual and dialect users, initially by English as a Second
Language specialists, has greatly increased the study of language itself.
Areas of study included in the teaching of English can cover why
languages and dialects exist, world languages and their connections,
the origins of writing, the evolution of English, English as a world
language, standard English and connections between language, class,
gender and race, and the effect of the mass media on attitudes to
language.

History
The contentious place of history as crucial to a non-racist multicultural
curriculum has already been touched on in this chapter. There is a
considerable literature discussing the political and nationalist bias in
history (Dance, 1960, 1971; Shah, 1988) but Her Majesty's Inspectors
have consistently noted the need to go beyond the teaching of a narrow
national idea of British history. In 1967, HMI published a pamphlet
Towards World History which asked 'If we have become part of one
world, . . . must we not concern ourselves with the history of that
world, as the only proper approach to understanding it?' (HMI, 1967),
and in 1971 they commented that 'local and national history must be

related to a wider context, not only in Europe, but in America, Africa and Asia' (HMI, 1978). A world history approach has the potential to promote global understanding, and as such has formed an important part of the *World Studies Project* (Hicks, 1987) whose materials are now used by over half the Local Education Authorities in England and Wales. History, as File (1984) has commented, provides opportunities for both analytical skills and a story of the past. The questions as to 'whose past?' and 'what past?' thus become important. In the 1980s many history teachers, in contrast to those education nationalists who asserted that there is an unproblematic British past to be taught, were searching for ways in which the history curriculum could present a more balanced view of Britain's imperial past, and more recent relations with the rest of the world. File has offered a series of positive ways in which topics and areas of study can lend themselves to cross-cultural historical analysis. He suggested a list of cross-national and non-white 'heroes and heroines' (File, 1984, p. 5) for those who still favour the 'personality' school of history which was put forward by the Board of Education in 1902 (see Finnemore, 1902).

How the history of Britain's imperial past is reinterpreted in the future will depend very much on the working group selected in January 1989 to advise the Secretary of State for Education as to how history should be taught in the national curriculum. The instructions to this group were that:

> The programmes of study should have at the core the history of Britain, the record of its past, and in particular, its political, constitutional and cultural heritage.

but the group was also to:

> take account of Britain's evolution and its changing role as a European, Commonwealth and world power.

Overall the group was required to:

> help pupils acquire and develop an historical approach based on objective analysis of evidence while remaining consistent with . . . the 1986 Education Act which prohibits political indoctrination.
>
> (Nash, 1989, p. 7)

The composition of the history working group[3] was criticized by the right-wing Centre for Policy Studies, which may indicate that some educational nationalists fear that broader global views of Britain's history might in future prevail.

The national curriculum
Until 1988 central government did not play a major role in decisions

about what to teach in schools. Control of the curriculum was shared between teachers, school governors, Local Education Authorities and examining bodies. The Department of Education and Science influenced the curriculum indirectly through publications giving advice and guidance, and through the activities of Her Majesty's Inspectors. Under the 1988 Education Act, central government took substantial control of the curriculum in all maintained schools. The national curriculum was intended to:

a. promote the spiritual, moral, cultural, mental and physical development of pupils at the school, and of society;
b. prepare such pupils for the opportunities, responsibilities and experiences of adult life. (Education Act, 1988, Section 1.2)

The three core, and seven foundation subjects, plus religious education, were intended to occupy at least 70 per cent of a school timetable; in the remaining time schools were to have discretion to offer other subjects or areas of experience. A task group on Assessment and Testing within the national curriculum was set up in 1987, and in December 1987 produced detailed levels of assessment to test what pupils had 'learned and mastered' at ages seven, eleven, fourteen and sixteen (Black, 1987).

By the time the Act became law in July 1988, many practitioners committed to multicultural educational change, and particularly those working in the Education Support Grant projects, were considering how to encompass, within a subject framework, the stated government intention to prepare all pupils for living in an ethnically diverse society. While it was discouraging that the Act made no reference to multicultural or non-racist education, it was encouraging that some development had already taken place in subject areas. The Secretary of State himself had suggested that such developments could be incorporated as cross-curricular themes and most secondary schools planned to continue with courses in personal and social education. These courses, singled out by the Hillgate Group and others as unnecessary, had become compulsory for all pupils in most secondary schools by the 1980s and were courses into which education for active citizenship and intercultural understanding could be fitted.

Immediate powers to suggest what should be incorporated into the core and foundation subjects lay with the working groups appointed by the Secretary of State. The mathematics proposals, produced in August 1988, included an explicitly anti-multicultural statement:

> It is sometimes suggested that the multicultural complexion of society demands a 'multicultural' approach to mathematics, with children being introduced to different number systems, foreign currencies and non-European measuring and counting devices. We are concerned that undue

emphasis on multicultural mathematics, in these terms, could confuse young children. Whilst it is right to make clear to children that mathematics is a product of diversity, priority must be given to ensuring that they have the knowledge, understandings and skills which they will need for adult life and employment in Britain . . . we have not therefore included any 'multicultural' aspects in any of our attainment targets.

(Department of Education and Science, 1988a, p. 87)

While these comments indicate a lack of knowledge as to what constitutes or could constitute multicultural mathematics, the dismissal of knowledge of different number and counting systems and foreign currencies is interesting. Independent schools, which are exempt from teaching the national curriculum, will certainly be teaching this kind of knowledge to pupils intending to be financial analysts, bankers, stockbrokers and the like. The comments also make the familiar and unsubstantiated assumption that multicultural aspects of mathematics are taught *instead of* the knowledge and skills needed for employment. The proposals did concede that some attention should be given to the history of mathematics showing the contribution of non-European countries.

The National Curriculum Council, after consulting some 435 organizations and individuals, produced a report on the mathematics proposals. This had nothing to say on the issue of multicultural mathematics, but noted that:

there will need to be further non-statutory guidance on cross-curricular matters, including issues relating to ethnic and cultural diversity.

(National Curriculum Council, 1988a)

However, in setting recommendations for attainment targets and examples of subject content, the Council report missed the opportunity for including cross-cultural mathematical examples, and gave no indication that mathematical contributions had come from non-European cultures.

The proposals from the science working party were much more positive. Under the heading 'Science and Cultural Diversity' the proposals stated:

Science education must take account of the ethnic and cultural diversity that the school population and society at large offers . . . the science curriculum must provide opportunities to help all pupils recognise that no one culture has a monopoly of scientific achievement. . . . It is therefore important that science books and other learning materials should include examples of people from ethnic minority groups working alongside others and achieving success in scientific work. Pupils should come to realise that the international currency of science is an important force for overcoming racial prejudice.

(DES, 1988b)

After consultation with over 400 organizations, the National Curriculum Council produced a science consultation report which was also very positively intercultural (National Curriculum Council, 1988b). A number of the attainment targets and programmes of study were specifically multicultural, and communication was singled out as an important cross-curricular theme. There were signs that a science curriculum in British schools in the 1990s would be able to encourage non-racist understandings and competence in working as equals among all pupils. The proposals from the English working group on *English for 5–11 year-olds*, published in November 1988, were also very positive. The components of the curriculum were to be Speaking, Listening, Reading and Writing, and the working group was particularly concerned that assessments in these components were fair and unbiased for all groups of pupils 'whether defined by ethnicity, gender or social class' (DES, 1988c). The proposals stated unequivocally that:

> A major assumption we are making is that the curriculum for all pupils should include informed discussion on the multicultural nature of British society, whether or not the individual school is culturally mixed. It is essential that the development of competence in spoken and written standard English is sensitive to the knowledge of other languages children might have . . . The large number of bilingual and biliterate children in the community should be seen as an enormous resource which ought to become more, not less, important to the British economy in the next few years.
>
> (*op. cit.*, p. 10)

The report very sensibly proposed that there should be both a 'cultural heritage' view of English which leads children to appreciate good English literature, and a 'cultural analysis' view helping children towards a critical understanding of the world they live in; 'children should know about the processes by which meanings are conveyed and about the way in which print and other media carry values' (p. 12). This kind of recommendation, if implemented, could ensure that pupils become aware of racist values and messages in the media. The proposals noted that English is part of an 'international discourse' and that while children should be introduced to a variety of literature:

> Formulations of 'literary tradition', 'our literary heritage' or lists of 'great works' may change over time.
>
> (*op. cit.*, p. 28)

Implementation of the full national curriculum will not be complete until well into the 1990s. Despite opposition there is considerable scope in all designated subjects, and in cross-curricular themes and activities, for ensuring that the curriculum becomes more appropriate for a modern multi-ethnic society.

Summary

This chapter has reviewed some attempts to change the content, approaches and underlying values of the curriculum, to make it more appropriate for an ethnically diverse, post-imperial society.

There has been no shortage of prescriptions as to what the aims of a multicultural, non-racist curriculum should be – the problems lie in implementing them. A damaging debate, which set up multicultural and anti-racist curriculum aims as antithetical, diverted attention from right-wing politically motivated critics, who by the late 1980s were having some success in marginalizing or vilifying any developments labelled multicultural, anti- or non-racist. Opposition became more vocal once it became apparent that change was being advocated in all schools, and that white areas would be affected. Opponents of multicultural and anti-racist education included important political figures, who have had some influence on the shape and content of the national curriculum. However, despite attempts to present multicultural curriculum activities as left-wing extremism, an examination of suggested changes in subject content and approaches would suggest that such changes are directed towards helping all pupils to develop intellectual skills, and the maturity, to examine the world in a more open-minded manner that many adults appear able to do. Proposals for Science and English, if not for mathematics, at least appear to be directed towards producing this kind of open-mindedness.

The following three chapters examine the Education Support Grant projects set up by the Secretary of State for Education, which were intended to further curriculum change and development in a multicultural, anti-racist direction.

Notes

1   The instructions of the Secretary of State for Education to the National Curriculum Council laid out in a letter sent in August 1988, were that the Council was to take account of the ethnic and cultural diversity in society and the need to promote equal opportunities.

2   Baroness Cox, who had considerable influence on the religious education clauses in the 1988 Education Act, is a member of a variety of influential, politically right-wing groups, including the Centre for Policy Studies, the Freedom Association and the Hillgate Group (see Gordon and Klug, 1986).

3   The Chair of the Working Group on History in the National Curriculum, appointed in January 1989 by the Secretary of State for Education is Commander Saunders-Watson, a recent President of the Historic House Association. Other members are

listed in Nash (1989). The Centre for Policy Studies complained that the group only contained one 'distinguished historian'.

Appendix to Chapter 4
Criteria for the selection of learning experiences

a   An insular curriculum, preoccupied with Britain and British values, is unjustifiable in the final quarter of the twentieth century. The curriculum needs to be both international in its choice of content and global in its perspective.

b   Contemporary British society contains a variety of social and ethnic groups; this variety should be made evident in the visuals, stories and information offered to children.

c   Pupils should have access to accurate information about racial and cultural differences and similarities.

d   People from British minority groups and from other cultures overseas should be presented as individuals with every variety of human quality and attribute. Stereotypes of minority groups in Britain and of cultures overseas, whether expressed in terms of human characteristics, life-styles, social roles or occupational status, are unacceptable and likely to be damaging.

e   Other cultures and nations have their own validity and should be described in their own terms. Wherever possible they should be allowed to speak for themselves and not be judged exclusively against British or European norms.

Source: Jeffcoate, R. (1976), 'Curriculum Planning in Multiracial Education', *Educational Research*, vol. 18, no. 3, pp. 192–200.

5 Education Support Grant projects

I want to encourage quality in education. I see Education Support Grants as a means to that end.

(Baker, 1987)

The Swann Committee believed that any meaningful progress towards re-orientating the curriculum in all schools in a more appropriate direction could not be done without adequate resources (DES, 1985, p. 358). Section 11 Grants, the major source of funding for activities in the multicultural area, were not thought appropriate for the new curriculum activities the committee was considering, although they did suggest that Section 11 be reviewed and through legislation made more appropriate to the needs of multiracial schools.[1] The committee believed that a major vehicle for ensuring that the curriculum could be suitably broadened was the Education (Grants and Awards) Act 1984, which allowed the government to pay Education Support Grants to Local Education Authorities for innovations and improvements in education. This short chapter documents the development of the Education Support Grant (ESG) projects, lists all the 'Educational Needs in a Multi-ethnic Society' projects funded by the Department of Education and Science between 1985 and 1988, discusses the nature of these projects and explains how a study of a selected sample of the projects came to be undertaken in 1987/88. The two following chapters describe the project work being undertaken in 24 Local Education Authorities.

The Education Support Grant programme

Education Support Grants were intended to be a special element in the contribution from central government towards the cost of education borne by Local Education Authorities. The ESG programme was initiated via the 1984 Education (Grants and Awards) Act, which empowered the Secretary of State to pay such grants. These grants were not intended to increase total LEA expenditure on education, but were to contribute 70 per cent of the expenditure for particular local projects approved by the DES. The scheme was modified by the

1986 Education (Amendments) Act, which limited the amount of support grant to 1 per cent of an LEA's expenditure on education. In 1988 the Secretary of State for Education decided that authorities should be encouraged to supplement public expenditure on certain ESG activities with contributions obtained from private sources, namely industry and commerce, parents and charities. 'An authority's willingness to elicit contributions will be one of the factors which he takes into account when he evaluates competing bids' (DES, 1987, p. 3).

According to DES officials, the purpose of the ESG programme was threefold:

☐ to encourage LEAs to target resources on educational problems which central government considered needed national solutions – 'in accordance with objectives of particular national importance' as a DES press release put it, and to encourage LEAs to respond swiftly to new demands on the education service;
☐ to assist teachers to exchange ideas and develop teaching materials; and
☐ to allow for experimental work.

The Secretary of State for Education, after consultation with interested parties, decided on the areas of activity to be supported, and he announced in June 1984 that a million pounds would be made available for 'pilot projects to meet the educational needs of people from ethnic minorities, to promote inter-racial harmony, or in other ways to prepare pupils and students for life in a multi-ethnic society'.[2]

LEAs were invited to put in proposals or 'bids' for projects in what eventually turned out to be 21 areas of 'national importance' and all projects had to receive DES approval. The 21 areas of activity which received grants in 1985/86 and 1986/87 ranged from 'Information Technology in Non-Advanced Further Education' to 'Mid-Day Lunch Time Supervision'. *Educational Needs in a Multi-ethnic Society* was only one of the 21 areas for which funds were made available in both the 1985/86 and 1986/87 round of 'bids' for support.

The level of expenditure for all projects in 1985/86 was £20 million of grant paid by central government on total expenditure of £29 million, and the planned level of expenditure for the following two years was £64 million of grant on an expenditure of £92 million. In reality, as projects varied in their running time from one to five years, expenditure already promised had to be considered and costs updated, and some bids for new activities in 1987/88 were not funded at all, including projects on educational needs in a multi-ethnic society. The amount of expenditure committed for 1988/89 was to be '£65.5 million at assumed 1988/89 prices leaving approximately £50 million for new starts' (DES, 1987). In April 1988 the Secretary of State announced in Parliament that he was proposing an expenditure of £125.5 million, which was heralded as a '£10 m rise in ESG funds' in the *Times Educational Supplement* (Hughill, 1988). In fact £48.5 million turned out to be partly money already promised earlier to continue on-going projects, and £77 million was mainly for projects and developments associated with the new 1988 Education Act. However, the amount did include expenditure on 49 more multi-ethnic projects.

ESG support for education in a multi-ethnic society

Because the DES had access to the Swann Report on the educational needs children from ethnic minorities before the report was published in March 1985, it had already been decided that one government response to Swann would be to invite LEAs to bid for ESG grants to support development work on educational needs for a multi-ethnic society. Since 1977, as noted in the Introduction to this book, central government policy has been directed towards broadening the commonly-held view that multicultural education is solely concerned with ethnic minorities. The encouragement of all LEAs, particularly those in all-white areas, to put in bids for ESG projects in the broad area of education for a multi-ethnic society, can be regarded as a continuation of a developing central policy. In addition, LEAs were encouraged to link their bids with the new arrangements made from 1986 for the grant-related in-service education of teachers (GRIST), under which training teachers for a multi-ethnic society became a national priority.[3] Invitations to LEAs to bid in the first round of projects produced some proposals which the DES considered were not properly thought through – perhaps understandably, given the short time-scale and lack of agreed criteria as to what would make a good project – and few of the first bids were for projects in all-white areas. In March 1986 a conference was organized by Her Majesty's Inspectors (HMI) at Buxton in Derbyshire, at which 'white' LEAs were specifically invited to put in proposals for projects. The number and costs of projects which were ultimately funded for Educational Needs in a Multi-ethnic Society is shown in the table below.

Table 1. *Number and costs of ESG projects for Educational Needs in a Multi-ethnic Society*

Year	Number of Projects Funded	Number of LEAs Involved	Approximate Cost
1985/86	35	25	£700,000
1986/87	35	32	£886,000
1987–88	no multi-ethnic projects funded		
1988/89	49	45	£1,392,421
	overall approximate total cost		£2,978,421

Thus between the years 1985 and 1988 119 projects were funded for varying lengths of time at the cost of about three million pounds, to undertake work on educational needs in a multi-ethic society. The projects, as can be established from Table 2, which lists all the projects by LEA and name, eventually covered almost every region in England (Welsh and Scottish projects are not included) and covered a wide variety of topics. Some LEAs whose 'bids' were not funded nevertheless found their own funds to allow the projects to be undertaken (two such projects are reported in the following chapters).

The projects funded from 1986 fall outside the scope of the study reported here, which visited a sample of projects begun in 1985 and 1986. The 1988 projects did include 33 in LEAs where there had previously been no projects – including such areas as the Isle of Wight, Isles of Scilly, Somerset, Cornwall, Suffolk, Norfolk, Oxfordshire, Cambridgeshire, Essex, Bedfordshire, Wirral, St Helens, Stockport, Knowsley, Sunderland and Northumberland. One project in Cheshire was withdrawn.

The description of projects from 1988 onwards are lengthier than previous projects and include much repetition of such phrases as 'enhancing awareness of Britain's ethnic diversity', 'promoting respect between pupils of different ethnic origins', 'reducing racial tensions', 'countering negative racial attitudes' and 'countering racial intolerance'. This is an indication that from 1988, projects were to be more firmly and openly directed towards changing the attitudes and behaviour of white pupils.

Projects were funded from 1985 and 1986 for periods of between one and five years, three being the median time, and from 1988 most projects were intended to run for three years to 1991. No further projects are envisaged by the DES, who have decided that future work in the multicultural area must now be included in the development of the national curriculum. The following table lists all the ESG projects by regional division. Project titles were intended to describe the actual work undertaken, but in some cases projects developed somewhat differently from their original description. Cost for the 1988 projects have been included to offer readers some idea of the variation in financial aid which was made available to different LEAs.

Table 2a. *Education Support Grants, 1985/86*
Educational Needs in a Multi-ethnic Society

LEA	Project description
Northern Division	
Rotherham	Co-ordination of Educational Support for Ethnic Minority Groups of Rotherham College of Arts and Technology.

Rotherham	Establishment of a Multi-Cultural Education Centre.
Humberside	Exchange visits between Humberside and Bradford schools.
Kirklees	Visits between Schools with High and Low % of Ethnic Minority children.
Kirklees	Team to Support Initiatives in Countering Racial harassment.
Bradford	Establishment of Working Party to Develop Ways of Supporting Learning of Bi-lingual Children.
Bradford	Exchange visits with Humberside Schools.
Bradford	Establishment of an Inter-faith Centre.
Leeds	Bringing Teenagers of Different Background together to Work on Joint Projects.
North Tyneside	Establishment of a Multicultural Resources Centre.
Sheffield	Commercial Studies Course for Black Young People.

North-West Division

Trafford	Twinning Schools with High and Low % of Ethnic Minority Pupils.
Tameside	Establishment of Community Language Centre.
Lancashire	Encouragement of Parental Involvement in Pre-School Education.
Manchester	Promoting Racial Harmony in Secondary Schools.

Midland Division

Walsall	Research into Extent and Nature of Racial Incidents.
Leicestershire	'Education Shop' to Provide Information about FE Courses.
Leicestershire	Race Awareness Training for FE College Staff.
Birmingham	Production of Materials for Teaching of Community Languages at Secondary Level.
Birmingham	Training Courses on School Management for Ethnic Minority Teachers.
Birmingham	Promotion of Racial Equality in Secondary Education.
Coventry	Extension of Specialist Youth Provision into Community-Run Institutions.
Coventry	Development of Religious Education and Humanities Curriculum.
Derbyshire	Team to Assist Schools in Raising Pupil Awareness of Ethnic Diversity.

Metropolitan and South Midland Division

Hillingdon	Bringing Children of Different Ethnic Background together in School Holidays.
Haringey	Establishment of Centre for Bilingualism.
ILEA	Expansion of Extended Day Programme for School Pupils.
ILEA	Short Business Courses Tailored to Needs of Ethnic Minorities.

Brent	Team to Develop Teaching Materials in Liaison with Community.
Southern Division	
Berkshire	Production of Videos Reflecting on Educational Issues of Relevance to Ethnic Minority Communities.
Berkshire	Race Awareness Training for Head Teachers.
Kent	Development of Multicultural Resource Centre.
Croydon	Team to Assist Schools: Introduction of Pupils to Ethnic Diversity.
South-West Division	
Gloucestershire	Team to Work with Teachers on Preparation of Pupils for Ethnic Diversity.

Table 2b. *Education Support Grants, 1986/87*
Educational Needs in a Multi-ethnic Society

LEA	Project description
Northern Division	
Bradford	Parental Outreach for Further Education.
Calderdale	Curriculum Development and INSET for Multi-ethnic Schools.
Cleveland	'Education for All' Curriculum Development and INSET.
Cumbria	'Education for All' Curriculum Development and ESL for Children Outside the Provision of Section 11.
Kirklees	Establishment of Multicultural Education Units in Two FE Colleges.
Leeds	Improving Race Relations in Schools and Youth Clubs.
North Tyneside	'Education for All' Curriculum Development in Schools and Colleges.
North Yorkshire	School Twinning and Initial and In-Service Teacher Training.
Sheffield	Support for Mother Tongue Classes.
North-West Division	
Lancashire	In-Service Teacher Training for Teachers from Multi-ethnic Schools.
Liverpool	Meeting the Needs of Ethnic Minority Students in FE.
Manchester	Promoting Mutual Understanding of Britain's Relationship with the Caribbean.
Wigan	'Education for All' Curriculum Development and INSET.
Midland Division	
Birmingham	Improving Race Relations in Primary Schools.
Birmingham	Asian Language Courses in FE for Beginners.
Coventry	Curriculum Development in the Humanities.

Derbyshire	School Partnership and Exchange Schemes.
Sandwell	Establishment of a Multicultural Resources Centre.
Shropshire	'Education for All' Curriculum Development, INSET and School Twinning.
Staffordshire	'Education for All' Curriculum Development, INSET and School Twinning.
Walsall	'Education for All' Curriculum Development and School Twinning.
Warwickshire	'Education for All' Curriculum Development, INSET and School Twinning.
Wolverhampton	Research into the Educational Needs of Ethnic Minority Students 16–19.

Eastern Division

Hertfordshire	Curriculum Development in RE.
Waltham Forest	Improving Race Relations in All-White Schools.

Metropolitan and South Midland Division

Ealing	Parental Liaison and Support for Mother Tongues in Primary Schools.
Harrow	Curriculum Development in Music.
ILEA	Outreach Scheme for FE for non-Section 11 Ethnic Minorities.
ILEA	Establishment of a 'Bengali Culture in Schools' Project.
Northamptonshire	Initial Teacher Training Provision to Meet Educational Needs in a Multi-Ethnic Society.
Northamptonshire	Resources Provision to Support 'Education for All' Curriculum Development and Mother Tongue Classes.

Southern Division

East Sussex	'Education for All' Curriculum Development and Inset.
Hampshire	'Education for All' Curriculum Development in Primary Schools. School Visits and Exchanges.
West Sussex	'Education for All' Curriculum Development. School Twinning.

South-West Division

Wiltshire	'Education for All' Curriculum Development. School Twinning.

Table 2c. *Education Support Grants, 1988/89*
Educational Needs in a Multi-ethnic Society

Note: an asterisk in the left hand column indicates that an LEA has not previously taken part in ESG activity.

LEA	Project description	Cost 1988/89 £
Northern Division		
Bradford	Development of learning resources to support subject-related ESL for pupils and students 16–19 in schools and colleges, and to improve race relations.	55,276
Doncaster*	Outreach work with the local ethnic minority community to improve basic literacy skills and increase takeup of FE and Adult Education Courses. To support Section 11 funded staff in schools and promote good practice.	22,539
Durham*	Curriculum development particularly in the Humanities to enhance awareness of Britain's ethnic diversity and reduce racial tension.	30,333
Gateshead*	Establishment of a Centre for Education Development and Research in a Multi-ethnic Society to support teachers working with ethnic minority pupils outside the scope of Section 11 (mainly Japanese) and in all-white schools and promote good practice.	29,162
Leeds	Continuation for a further two years of a Neighbourhood Link Youth Project funded under the 1985–86 ESG Programme. The project brings together young people from the majority and minority communities for joint activities and is designed to reduce racial tension.	25,904
Northumberland*	Establishment of a Curriculum Project Team to work with classroom teachers and their pupils age 8–14 to produce INSET and teaching materials on attitudes, prejudice and stereotyping with particular reference to multi-ethnic issues in a mono-ethnic community.	30,384
South Tyneside*	Establishment of a Multi-Cultural Education Resource Centre/Library to support curriculum development.	17,016

Sunderland*	Curriculum development to improve race relations and present a more positive image of a plural society.	not known
Wakefield	Purchase of teaching materials, resources and equipment to support INSET courses funded under the Traditional Urban Programme. (This earlier project was transferred from ESG to TUP under a special arrangement for 1986–87 only.)	52,000

North-West Division

Bolton*	Establishment of a Multi-Cultural Resources Centre to build up materials to support the work of Section 11 funded staff.	41,218
Knowsley*	Curriculum development and INSET for multi-cultural education in the primary sector, using a cross-curricular approach.	33,366
Lancashire	Pre-School support for ethnic minority parents and children through the purchase of resources to extend the work of Section 11 funded Home/School Liaison Teachers.	12,376
Manchester	Purchase of resources and equipment to support the work of Section 11 staff in schools and colleges.	30,337
Oldham*	Development of school-twinning schemes and work with older children and young people to improve racial attitudes.	54,412
Rochdale	Curriculum development to equip pupils and students for life in a multi-ethnic society and promote racial harmony.	28,948
Salford*	Establishment of a Multi-Cultural Resource Centre to support work including ESL teaching to pupils and adults, preparation and translation of information booklets for ethnic minority parents and curriculum development and INSET for multi-cultural education.	28,803
St Helens*	Work at St Helens College of FE to promote curriculum change and raise awareness of staff and students to the issues related to life and work in a multi-ethnic society.	39,270
Stockport*	Curriculum development to enhance awareness and understanding of ethnic diversity and promote racial harmony.	20,438
Wirral*	Curriculum development to promote understanding and respect for people of different ethnic and cultural origins and to raise teacher expectations of ethnic minority pupils.	30,160

Midland Division

Dudley*	Establishment of a Saturday School for Afro-Caribbean pupils with individual learning programmes so as to reduce underachievement and raise teacher expectations.	24,440
Leicestershire	Support for the work of Section 11 funded staff through the purchase of computers to assist ESL teaching and other resource materials.	26,661
Nottinghamshire*	Curriculum development and INSET to enhance awareness and understanding of ethnic diversity.	18,787
Sandwell	Provision of INSET and purchase of materials to support and increase the effectiveness of Section 11-funded teachers in schools.	23,733
Walsall	Extension of the MSC/FEU [Further Education Unit] project on 'Equal Opportunities for Ethnic Minorities in Work-Related NAFE' [National Adult and Further Education], through outreach work with ethnic minorities, staff development and improved careers guidance.	41,621

Eastern Division

Bedfordshire*	Curriculum development, particularly in the Humanities, to promote mutual understanding and respect between pupils of different ethnic origins.	31,304
Cambridgeshire*	Cross-curricular development to promote and extend education for ethnic diversity in a pyramid of all white schools. Purchase of materials to support Section 11-funded staff in multi-ethnic schools and colleges. INSET for staff in FE colleges.	52,000
Essex*	Establishment of a Multi-Cultural Resources Centre providing in-school support and INSET to enhance awareness and understanding of Britain's ethnic diversity.	30,370
Hertfordshire	Investigation of the educational needs of the Bangladeshi community in St Albans and development of courses to meet those needs, in accordance with the recommendations of the HAC Report 'Bangladeshis in Britain'.	25,220
Newham*	Establishment of a unit to support and coordinate the work of out-reach teachers funded under Section 11, to reduce incidents of racial harassment in schools and promote good practice in race relations.	27,040

Norfolk*	Curriculum development to prepare all pupils for life in a multi-ethnic society and counter racial intolerance and discrimination.	30,334
Redbridge*	Purchase of resource materials to support the work of Section 11-funded teachers in primary and special schools. Curriculum development and INSET in mainly white primary schools to promote racial harmony and prepare pupils for life in a multi-ethnic society.	28,444
Suffolk*	Curriculum development and materials production to enhance awareness and understanding of Britain's ethnic diversity and counter negative racial attitudes.	30,160
Waltham Forest	Development and evaluation of materials to support the work of Section 11-funded staff.	11,440

Metropolitan and South Midland Division

Enfield*	INSET to increase teachers' understanding of the background and experience of the ethnic minority pupils in their school, raise teacher expectations of such pupils and reduce underachievement through a review of the curriculum and teaching methods.	27,321
Haringey	Purchase of teaching materials and equipment to support staff working with Bangladeshi pupils and students in primary and secondary schools and youth and adult education. (A bid for Section 11 funding for the staff involved is the subject of a concurrent application to the Home Office.)	37,440
Hounslow*	Mother tongue support and the provision of resources to enhance the early learning of bilingual pupils. Any differences in linguistic and conceptual development between bi-lingual 4-year olds receiving support in both English and mother-tongue and those receiving support in English only, will be quantified by research.	25,056
ILEA	INSET to improve arrangements for pastoral care in schools to make them more responsive to the needs of ethnic minority pupils. Issues of academic achievement will be addressed, as well as personal and social development.	13,520

Northamptonshire	Provision of a Multi-Cultural Advisory and Educational Resource Unit in the Adult Education Service to re-inforce the work of Section 11-funded staff, particularly in ESL and Adult Literacy, and promote mutual understanding and respect between people of different ethnic origins.	18,616
Oxfordshire*	Work with both mono- and multi-racial schools to assist their response to the LEA's discussion document 'Prejudice and Equality'. It will involve analysis, preparation and implementation of plans for future action, and monitoring and evaluation of progress.	28,860

Southern Division

Berkshire	Establishment of a study skills centre open after school and at weekends, to provide additional support for Afro-Caribbean pupils following GCSE courses, so as to reduce underachievement. Careers guidance and advice on FHE courses will also be provided.	33,280
Hampshire	Development of a Central Resource Centre and smaller resource bases at the ESL and Teachers Centre to support ethnic minority pupils and prepare all pupils and students for life in a multi-ethnic society.	36,816
Isle of Wight*	INSET and curriculum development to increase awareness of Britain as a multicultural society.	32,552
Richmond*	Curriculum development and INSET to enhance teachers' understanding of the background and experience of ethnic minority pupils and raise expectations of their potential, and to promote in all white schools understanding and respect for pupils of different ethnic origin.	35,776
Surrey*	Curriculum development and INSET to enhance teachers' understanding of the background and experience of ethnic minority pupils and raise expectations of their potential, and to promote in schools and colleges generally understanding and respect for those of different ethnic origin.	33,644
Sutton*	Curriculum development and INSET to promote racial harmony, meet the needs of ethnic minority pupils and prepare all pupils for life in a multi-ethnic society.	13,788

South-West Division

Cornwall*	Curriculum development, INSET, and resource provision to enhance awareness and understanding of Britain's ethnic diversity.	30,198
Isles of Scilly*	Purchase of teaching materials and resources to enhance awareness of Britain's ethnic diversity.	1,040
Somerset*	Establishment of a Multi-Ethnic Education Unit to enhance awareness, understanding and appreciation of Britain's ethnic diversity through curriculum development and INSET.	30,618
Wiltshire	Establishment of a Multi-Cultural Resource Centre to support the work of Section 11 funded staff.	10,400

Source: These project lists were supplied by the Department of Education and Science.

Criteria for selection of projects

Initially little guidance was available to LEAs on the criteria which, in the opinion of DES, would make for a successful project. Eventually more advice was offered by DES on criteria for selection. Some of these were as follows:

☐ LEAs were to make sure projects were viable, in terms of size, staffing and finance.

☐ Projects were to indicate their aims and objectives and (on paper) demonstrate they could achieve these.

☐ Projects should be practically consistent – and supported by the LEA. There was, according to DES, some evidence that a few projects did not have the whole-hearted support of their LEAs, and some projects found difficulty in recruiting suitably qualified staff, particularly for short-term projects. LEAs were eventually advised to pay staff at advisory teacher level. It was clear that DES hoped that projects would recruit experienced, enthusiastic staff who could not only innovate but also influence colleagues.

☐ Projects were to be innovative, but this would be relative to how far the LEA had developed its multicultural educational activity. Examples of innovative activities likely to receive DES support were dual LEA projects, i.e. bids put in jointly by two authorities, and bids for twinning of schools in areas of high and low ethnic minority settlement.

☐ All projects were to have some form of internal evaluation built in, although the form this should take was not specified. The DES required all projects to give in an annual progress report and HMI were to visit all projects regularly. It was also suggested that all projects create a steering or a management committee and that local HMI be involved. There was no requirement that external evaluators of projects be appointed, although some did make such appointments.

The titles of the projects give an indication that funding has been awarded for what can be broadly described as curriculum development, production of materials, in-service teacher training, changing pupil attitudes, inter-ethnic exchanges, and specific projects such as setting up multicultural resource or inter-faith centres.

All the projects visited for this present study mentioned the publication of the Swann Report (DES, 1985a) as a rationale for their project work, and some LEAs, encouraged by DES, anticipated Swann and wrote bids for projects before the publication of the report. The major message of the Swann Report – that *all* pupils needed to be offered a good, relevant and up-to-date education for life in a multiracial, multicultural Britain and a changed world, undoubtedly acted as a catalyst in pushing policy-makers and practitioners towards a focus on 'all-white' areas. The impressive amount of supporting statements for 'Education for All' – the Department of Education and Science, Her Majesty's Inspectorate, the Schools Council, the Council for National Academic Awards, the Teachers' Unions, academics, and a variety of other interested parties – did bring into the wider public domain discussion as to why and how the curriculum could be changed 'to develop a broader, multicultural perspective to the curriculum and seek to counter the influence of racism' (p. 345).

It has already been noted however, that a movement to reform a 'curriculum appropriate to our Imperial past' had been in existence for some years before the Swann Committee was constituted. The movement was supported at first by a relatively small number of practitioners but eventually found its way into national and local policy statements (Tomlinson, 1983). The focus for this movement continued, in the 1980s, to be mainly in schools with ethnic minority pupils, white areas being slow to accept the need for change. The Swann Report noted the difficulty of finding examples of 'good practice' in all-white schools (p. 327) and welcomed the announcement of the ESG projects, in June 1984, as a means by which all LEAs and schools could 're-appraise the extent to which the curriculum which they offer to pupils is relevant to the nature of contemporary British Society, and to explore ways in which a broader, pluralist perspective which seeks in particular to counter the influence of racism, can be incorporated into existing provision' (p. 361). There is no doubt that by the late 1980s the ESG projects have provided examples of 'good practice' which the Swann Committee found lacking in the early part of the decade.

Background to the study

The study of a sample of ESG projects developed from the annual conference of the National Anti-Racist Movement in Education in

1987, which was organized on the theme of 'Anti-Racist Education in All-White Areas'. A session at this conference was offered by the workers on the Wiltshire ESG 'Education for All' project, and this was the first occasion on which other workers on similar ESG projects had been able to meet together and discuss their approaches and experiences. After the conference the project workers formed an ESG network and agreed to share information on the development of their various projects – which were spread around the country from Cumbria to Croydon – and to offer mutual support for what were, in some cases, turning out to be difficult undertakings. The workers also agreed to hold conferences, four being held in June 1987, March 1988, July 1988, and March 1989.

The study of a sample of projects was primarily intended to provide information for ESG project workers and other interested parties, on the kind of work being attempted in the projects and to be an analysis of the aims, methods of working, and effects, of carrying out projects relating to educational needs for a multi-ethnic society, in predominantly all-white areas.

Between October 1987 and March 1988 visits were made to 18 projects in England which had obtained ESG grants for work in white areas, and also to two projects which were in operation supported wholly by the local authority – the initial bid having 'failed'. Written information was collected from four more projects. Visits were made to, and information collected from, projects in the following LEAs: Wiltshire, Cumbria, Shropshire, Manchester, Walsall, Wigan, West Sussex, Kirklees, Waltham Forest, North Tyneside, Staffordshire, North Yorkshire, Cleveland, Warwickshire, Humberside, Northamptonshire, Derbyshire, Newcastle upon Tyne, Oldham, East Sussex, Hertfordshire, Kent, Croydon and a national resource centre based in Berkshire.[4]

The workers appointed to the projects were asked to describe their project in the following terms:

☐ location, contact address, starting date, staffing, funding and management;

☐ aims, short and long-term objectives, methods of working and any materials produced, content of in-service programmes and any pupil programmes;

☐ methods of evaluation, and positive effects noted on teachers, pupils, other LEA personnel, parents and community, and any negative effects noted on same plus any general comments on the work.

Interviews with workers were written up and returned for checking. Several projects returned the accounts with minor amendments and those quoted here have signified that they were willing to share information about their work. Some workers, who felt that their work involved such sensitive issues, or wished to keep a 'low profile', were occasionally reluctant to have their work made public and several projects which were approached for visiting signified that they were already in the process of evaluating and writing-up work they had been involved in, for presentation to a wider audience. On the visits to the projects requests were made for illustrative materials – curriculum materials developed, details of INSET courses, reports, papers and newsletters produced, any LEA policies etc. – not to make any comprehensive collection, but to provide an illustrative flavour of the projects. A very small amount of this material is included in the following chapters and a short bibliography of materials, including some articles published by project workers, is appended to this chapter. The projects are described in the order in which they were visited. Projects on educational needs for a multi-ethnic society were funded from 1985 and 1986 for periods of between one and five years. Those reported on here all started during these years, but, at the time of writing, had been in operation for varying lengths of time, some are well-developed, some barely started, and there were wide variations in staffing and resources; one project had one staff member, another 20! The projects had varying levels of support from their LEAs and from other colleagues; a few were attempting to operate in relatively hostile climates. Some projects were able to work in collaboration and cooperation with existing LEA multicultural or bilingual support services (usually funded under Section 11) and several projects had been overtaken by general multicultural developments in their authorities. The one-off nature of the visits means that the material presented here can only be regarded as a 'snap-shot' – a description at a particular moment in time – of the projects. All the projects are 'continuous developments', the expectation by DES being that local authorities will continue to fund projects after ESG funding finishes. DES also expected that project work would be disseminated into other schools in the various authorities. Indeed, a major rationale for the existence of all the projects is that curriculum development work and teacher expertise should be taken into the mainstream of education.

Evaluation and dissemination

At the outset of the ESG programme there was considerable variation in the specified evaluation strategies for the various activities. Some kinds of projects were required to take part in national evaluation schemes. For example, *Information Technology in Schools* projects 'will be evaluated through a national evaluation project, returns from LEA's, further DES statistical surveys, and by general inspection'

(DES, 1987, p. 32). By contrast, all that was required of projects on *Education for a Multi-ethnic Society* was that LEAs should supply a description of how projects were to be monitored and evaluated at local level (*op. cit.*, p. 9) and arrange for annual reports of each project to go to the DES. This gave the strong impression that DES considered some activities more important than others in terms of the evaluation required. Projects on education for a multi-ethnic society were either not sufficiently important to be nationally evaluated or they were regarded as too contentious to draw attention to by national evaluation.

A similar situation was observable over the dissemination of the project work. No arrangements were made by the DES to disseminate project work on education for a multi-ethnic society between Local Education Authorities. This, as chapter seven indicates, became a source of considerable frustration to project workers, who did not wish to 're-invent the wheel' and would have valued some formal links and dissemination of developments between projects. It was left to enthusiastic project workers to create their own informal networks, start up newsletters and run conferences, although the DES did capitalize on the work done by inviting workers to discuss their projects at DES regional courses.[5]

Notes

1 The government published a consultative document setting out a new form of Grant under Section 11 (Local Government Act 1966) on 1978. This resulted in a Local Government Grants (Ethnic Groups) Bill, which never became law as it failed to pass through Parliament before the General Election of 1979.

2 DES Press Notice, 95/84, 12/6/84.

3 In-service training of teachers for a multi-ethnic society ceased to be a national priority in 1988.

4 Sixteen of the projects were visited solely by Peter Coulson, the Wigan teacher-fellow seconded to Lancaster University, 1987/88.

5 A DES regional course was held at the Roehampton Institute of Higher Education in September 1988 on the theme of Multi-ethnic Education in White Areas. Project workers from Cumbria, Wiltshire and Manchester contributed to the course.

Appendix to Chapter 5

Selected Bibliography Related to ESG Projects in 'White Areas'
Articles written by ESG workers:

BROWN, C., 1988, 'The White Highlands: anti-racism?', *Multicultural Teaching*, vol 6, no 2.

CHAUHAN, C., 1988, 'Anti-Racist Education in All-White Areas: a black perspective', *Multicultural Teaching*, vol 6, no 2.

DENT, R., 1988, *Faith of Our Fathers. Roman Catholic Schools in a Multi-Faith Society*, Coventry, City of Coventry Education Department.

MOULD, W., 1986, 'No Rainbow Coalition on Tyneside', *Multicultural Teaching*, vol 4, no 3.

NATIONAL ANTI-RACIST MOVEMENT IN EDUCATION, 1987, *Anti-Racist Movement in Education: Conference Report*, Walsall, West Midlands.

PATEL, K., *ESG Network*, newsletter no 1, May 1988.

SHARMA, S., 1987, 'Education for All on Wheels – the intercultural mobile unit', *Multicultural Teaching*, vol 5, no 2.

SPENCER, D., 1988, 'Trial and Error Approach to Anti-Racist Education', *Times Education Supplement*, 6.5.88.

WHITE, N., 1987, 'New Resources for All-White Area', *Multicultural Teaching* vol 6, no 1.

A small selection of useful material available from or produced by projects, to indicate that all projects now have material which could be made more widely available, is listed below:

Cumbria LEA, 1987, *Education for Life in a Multicultural Society*, Curriculum Paper no. 14.

Cumbria ESG Project, *Starting with Ourselves – towards multicultural education*, a videotape.

Derbyshire County Council, 1987, *Towards The 1990s*, An action programme for Derbyshire County Council for Education for All People in Derbyshire.

Manchester ESG Project, 1987, *Inside-Outside: an evaluation document;* includes videos of project work.

Walsall ESG Project, 1987, *Asian Names*, a guide to help people understand the naming system of people from the Asian sub-continent.

Warwickshire LEA, 1987, *Curriculum Guidelines: Inter-cultural education for all*.

Wiltshire LEA, 1987, *Mathematics for All*.

6 A description of the Education Support Grant projects

This chapter describes 23 ESG projects concerned with education for a multi-ethnic society visited between October 1987 and March 1988. The information presented is that offered by project staff at the time of the visits, although some activities and publications subsequently reported are included. The visits are reported in more detail in Tomlinson and Coulson (1988).

All the projects were asked who, in their Local Education Authority, had initiated the project and written the bid for ESG money from the DES. The list below summarizes the replies:

Project initiators	Number
Chief/Senior Advisor/Group of Advisors	5
Advisor/Inspector for Multicultural Education	13
Education Officer/Head of Multicultural Service	3
Education Committee	2

Advisors appear to have been the major catalyst for the project bids, and the major source of support once they were in operation. In almost every case, project workers spoke warmly of the help they had received from advisors who had written bids, persuaded colleagues to support them, and given active support. Once the projects were operating, a crucial factor in making them viable was the level of the support given by senior and advisory staff. Workers[1] felt that to be really successful a project should have the full support of the chief education officer, his officers and the elected members. The DES had suggested that all projects should have a steering committee and 15 projects reported having guidance from such a group or committee. The most extensive example comprised the Heads of the schools involved, teacher representatives, the multicultural education advisor, the chief advisor, the project evaluator, representatives from the local church, a minority representative and a parent governor. Other steering groups had fewer members. In four projects a teachers' working group acted as a guide and support and in three cases workers had created a self-managing group.

The existence of an LEA policy document or guidelines on multicultural education was considered by workers to contribute to the success of the project. Sixteen LEAs had such policies, four did not and three had policies in production.

The following is a list of the projects analysed.

Wiltshire
Name: Education For All ESG Project
Duration: September 1988–89
Staff: Three full-time workers
Funding: ESG
Location: A Salisbury middle school
Coverage: 15 first and three middle schools, one 13–18 year compre-
            hensive school

Aims   To develop a greater awareness of the multicultural nature of society through the curriculum and institutional arrangements in schools, to explore ways of using curricular opportunities in all subject areas, to promote understanding of racial justice and equality, to work with teachers to challenge racial hostility in all its forms, to encourage teachers to develop positive attitudes to ethnic minorities.

Methods   The project was linked to the county curriculum policy and involved mathematics and science advisors and local HMI. Mathematics, a 'high status' subject, became a deliberate focus for the first year's work. Demonstration weeks of maths teaching were organized and a collaborative teaching contract with class teachers was drawn up. Curriculum development in art, music, drama, humanities and personal and social education was established and the project produced a newsletter to keep teachers informed of developments.

Materials and Pupil Programmes   A multicultural mathematics week was organized and *Mathematics For All* (Wiltshire LEA, 1988) published – a book with work for pupils which included Vedic number work, cross-cultural number systems and multiplication, tangrams, Rangoli and Islamic patterns and instructions for a Maths Trail starting from a local church. A project on the art and culture of Nigeria was organized, including a visit from a Nigerian artist-in-residence at the Commonwealth Institute. Work on Divali was requested by one school and became a topic across the curriculum and it led to twinning with a Southampton school to perform drama from the Ramayana. A social education unit on 'Values' was developed which included a role-playing exercise on 'Planning permission for the siting of a mosque'.

In-Service   Project workers contributed to the school-based in-service and organized workshops in their project schools for 10 teachers per session. INSET (in-service education for teachers) papers and pre-reading lists were given to participants, the videos *Black* and *Recognising Racism* and role-playing were used to introduce discussion of prejudice and stereotyping.

Comments and Effects The workers kept personal diaries and evaluated the effects of the project on pupils, who found the work new, interesting and challenging. Widespread appreciation of the work by local teachers was the biggest success and advisors across the curriculum began to recognize the relevance of the initiatives. Negative effects included the well-publicized antagonism of a local councillor (see chapter four), articles in the *Daily Mail* and the *Sun* accusing the project of 'banning toadstools and teddy bears' (*Sun*, 2.3.87) and some 'hate' mail.

Cumbria
Name: Cumbria Multicultural Education project
Duration: January 1987–90
Staff: One full-time curriculum development officer and, from January 1988, two advisory teachers
Funding: ESG and local authority GRIST (grant related in-service training) money
Location: Area education office, Whitehaven
Coverage: No specific schools – the approach was to support Cumbria teachers who had begun to take initiatives in a multicultural and anti-racist direction

Aims To build up teacher awareness of multicultural education as a 'good education', to challenge racial inequality and promote equal opportunity, and to co-ordinate individual initiatives.

Methods The worker responded to teacher requests for help and advice, encouraged a network of interested teachers and produced a newsletter to share information. She joined the sub-committee of a working group on multicultural education to produce *Education for Life in a Multicultural Society* (Cumbria LEA, 1987), writing sections on 'Needs, Implications, Actions and Support' intended to give teachers starting points for the development and evaluation of good practice. She supported a multicultural pilot project in Kendal which involved six schools – one nursery, three primary and two secondary – during which there were exchange visits with schools in Liverpool, Lancashire and Sheffield and she supported bilingualism for the few minority pupils in the area, linked to work on linguistic prejudice with white teachers.

Materials and Pupil Programmes A video *Starting with ourselves* . . .

towards multicultural education was produced with the TV unit of Carlisle Art College and made available for hire. The project worker resisted building up a resource centre, preferring to concentrate on changing teacher attitudes.

In-Service　The worker contributed to conferences organized by the Education Department and the local College of Higher Education and responded to requests for whole-school, in-service days or seminars. In September 1987 the Cumbria policy statement on multicultural education and the curriculum paper were launched at a primary headteachers meeting (see *Appendix 1* to this chapter for *Questions for Discussion* at this meeting).

Comments and Effects　The idea of multicultural, anti-racist education was relatively new in Cumbria and awareness of the issues was still low in the county as a whole. By 1988 there were many good examples of individual work and teachers reported that the work 'made them think'. Some defensive reactions were observed and a few teachers took a missionary attitude to others. The most positive effect was that without the project, multicultural education would probably not have been regarded as a serious issue for policy making, resources and teacher training.

Shropshire
Name:　　　 Education for a Multi-Ethnic Society
Duration: January 1987–August 1989
Staff:　　　 Two full-time workers
Funding:　ESG
Location:　Education office, Shrewsbury
Coverage: County-wide but initially centred on allocated schools in the Oswestry area

Aims　To raise awareness of the issues of a multicultural society, especially racism, to run a resource centre, support teachers, produce a portfolio of good practice, encourage an LEA policy and foster links with black community groups in Telford.

Methods　The workers undertook collaborative training and gave advice on a multicultural dimension in the project schools, and prepared resource packs of teaching materials. Work was concentrated in eight primary schools some of which were, initially, unwilling participants. Workers also supported multi-ethnic schools in Telford offering guidelines on religious observance, community languages, food, dress and holidays, and helped arrange exchange visits with urban West Midlands schools, centring the visits around science work.

Materials and Pupil Programmes　Packs of discussion materials were produced for distribution to all Shropshire schools and school governors. Materials and resources for schools were collected in the Resource Centre in Shrewsbury.

In-Service An in-service programme of two-day courses was offered county-wide covering issues of race and racism, the meaning of multicultural education, world studies, and learning through languages. An initial attempt to train senior staff only, was abandoned. The successful model for in-service work developed in one area is shown in *Appendix 2* to this chapter. Training seminars were also organized for the Schools Library Service, the Hospital and Home Tuition Service and for advisors.

Comments and Effects The workers reported that pupils had responded with enthusiasm to the new curriculum developments, but the effect on teachers was less easy to assess, those who were antagonistic remained so and there was a report of upper secondary school lessons degenerating into a 'platform for racism'. Raising the awareness of advisors and advisory teachers was the major success and parents had been helpful about exchange visits, although one governor and a local vicar had opposed a visit to a predominantly Muslim class. Organized racist activity in the Ludlow area during 1987 had led to the South Shropshire Youth Service developing an anti-racist policy.

Manchester
Name: ESG Multicultural Project
Duration: September 1985–1988
Staff: One full-time director/coordinator, one administrative assistant and a part-time researcher, video technician and youth worker
Funding: ESG. The LEA undertook to disseminate materials after the project finished but financial problems affected this commitment
Location: Teachers Centre, Didsbury
Coverage: An 11–18 comprehensive school, two feeder primary schools and a youth club

Aims To promote multicultural and anti-racist education in mainly white schools; to produce teaching materials and strategies to this end and to develop in-service training on issues of anti-racism.

Methods The project developed a teacher-led approach. Ideas, support and materials were offered to interested teachers and the director organized outside visits from poets and playwrights. The use of arts in schools was a most successful strategy. A Birmingham theatre group was invited to school and the sixth-form General Studies class watched a performance of poetry and music by 'African Dawn', then held a session on racism with the actors. Individual teachers made changes to their subject presentation and examination courses, for example, the home economics group developed workshops with The Caribbean Craft circle. A newsletter for schools was started but abandoned when it produced no response from teachers. A staff support group was formed in the secondary school.

Materials and Pupil Programmes   Drama workshops on the prejudiced attitudes of fourth-year pupils developed into a play *Inside-Outside* with help from a playwright and a theatre group. The play and an evaluation have been published (Manchester ESG Project, 1987). Video records of workshops and artists in schools were produced and made available to other schools and an 'International Evening' was organized successfully.

In-Service   The Director was made a member of the Secondary Schools Academic Board and worked with secondary teachers in small groups to produce case studies of good classroom practice. Anti-racist staff development workshops were started for primary Heads and teachers, using outside speakers, the video *Black*, work on designing school policies, and small group anti-racist work.

Comments and Effects   The work took on an added impetus after the murder of an Asian pupil at a nearby school in September 1986, and the anti-racist work of Manchester LEA came to national attention. The report of the Inquiry into the murder praised the Manchester ESG project for its positive effects in white schools (Spencer, 1988). The Director felt that by concentrating on four schools the work had had positive impact on the pupils, particularly the drama work. Teachers had begun to think issues through and understood the concept of curriculum permeation better. The project collaborated well with the local inspectorate, especially in English, Maths and Home Economics, but had an 'uneasy working relationship' with the city administration.

Walsall
Name: ESG Multicultural project
Duration: January 1980 – December 1988
Staff: Three full-time workers
Funding: ESG
Location: Large, 'nearly white' comprehensive school
Coverage: Other Walsall schools and the local community

Background   The borough was an area of ethnic minority settlement and since 1982 had been sensitive to the need to change the curriculum and attitudes in its schools. There had been clear evidence of racist incidents and antagonistic attitudes of white pupils, long term hostility to a local travellers' site and a developing National Front presence in the area.

Aims To collect and document data on racial attitudes in schools and of pupils, parents and the local community; to monitor the nature and frequency of racial incidents in schools; to set up school working parties and help them draft appropriate codes of practice; to bring about closer contacts between schools and the local community.

Methods The workers saw themselves as action researchers working to stimulate change. However, during the first year they kept a low profile and produced multicultural support material. They carried out a research project in schools, with teacher cooperation, exploring the racial attitudes of children aged 4–13 years, and held in-depth interviews with white people in neighbourhood offices to establish attitudes to the local area and to black people. They also developed questionnaires – one for teachers on racist name-calling in schools and one on the racial attitudes of the unemployed. Some team teaching on 'Reducing racial prejudice' had been undertaken in personal and social education courses at secondary schools. A regular newsletter was produced for all authority schools.

Materials Produced The team produced booklets on Divali and Eid and on Asian names (Walsall ESG Project, 1987). Research materials, using photographs, for use with young children were developed.

In-Service The authority allocated compulsory in-service training days to issues of racial harmony, which were planned jointly with the Travellers' Service through a working party which became permanent. The training days helped teachers to recognize racist incidents and work on codes of practice for responses to incidents.

Comments and Effects This project was evaluated externally by the Department of Education, the University of Warwick. Its effects appeared to be positive, bringing out issues which many people would prefer to ignore, although it was difficult to evaluate long-term effects on the pupils. Strong support had come from the DES and the LEA.

Wigan
Name: Educational Needs in a Multi-Ethnic Society
Duration: September 1986 –July 1989
Staff: One worker to July 1987, thereafter two
Funding: ESG to April 1987, then LEA GRIST funds
Location: Teachers Centre
Coverage: All authority primary schools

Aims To give teachers in all-white primary schools an awareness and understanding of the multi-ethnic nature of British society; to organize a programme of in-service training; to research teacher attitudes.

Methods and In-Service The first worker selected 25 primary schools to research attitudes to multicultural education and to in-service training in this area. Two schools declined to participate and a 'defensive parochialism' was evident in others. The second worker spent two days per week at Lancaster University, researching other ESG projects, and helped organize the in-service work. All schools were invited to send teachers to two-day or five-day courses, with supply cover provided, and 100 teachers attended, from 61 schools. An evaluation of this work led to the formation of a teacher support group for curriculum change, another for nursery teachers, a series of evening open meetings and collaboration with the LEA Equal Opportunities group. Some resource material was collected and loaned to schools but the team preferred to concentrate on attitude change. The in-service courses in 1986–88 concentrated on media studies, religious education, multicultural arts, racism awareness, whole school policies, school libraries, racial incidents in white primary schools and moral education through multicultural assemblies.

Materials and Pupils Programmes Teacher working groups developed materials on 'An approach to Harvest' and 'The Story of Martin Luther King'. In December 1986 the coordinator produced a detailed evaluation of teacher response to visits and questionnaires. 80 per cent agreed that pupils should be prepared for life in a multi-ethnic society, but 32 per cent did *not agree* that Britain was a multi-ethnic society while 22 per cent felt it was normal for white children to feel threatened by black people (Vickers, 1986).

Comments and Effects Pupils were interested and motivated by the curriculum work but it was unclear how far this reflected a change in attitude to black people. One pupil commented 'My uncle says we should be learning about our own religion' after a visit to a Hindu temple. The team felt the in-service programme was a major success and had 'fired a nucleus of teachers with enthusiasm' but some teachers felt the work was 'another bandwagon' and some affirmed their belief that society was monocultural. The workers were grateful for advisory support but regretted the lack of an LEA multicultural policy as back-up for their work.

West Sussex
Name: Multicultural Education Project
Duration: September 1986 – March 1988
Staff: One advisory teacher for multicultural education (who had an interest in development education and world studies)
Funding: ESG for one year, then LEA
Location: West Sussex Professional Centre
Coverage: Six pilot schools – four primary, one 8–12 years, one 5–13 years plus 'outreach' work with other schools and advisors

Background The ESG work was seen as a way to fulfil the LEA commitment to develop a curriculum relevant to the modern world. It complemented the agreed syllabus for multifaith religious education and the existing European and international links in the authority.

Aims To heighten teacher awareness of education as a means of preparing pupils to respect each other; to examine ways in which the primary and lower secondary curriculum could be enriched by the development of multicultural dimensions; to develop, test and disseminate new materials.

Methods The worker organized whole school meetings or worked with individual teachers to develop new ideas. In one school, an enthusiastic teacher gradually encouraged colleagues to join her in working on food and dance topics. An informal network of teacher support and self-help was encouraged and links formed with other advisors.

Materials and Pupil Programmes A media initiative on 'Images' was successfully developed. One school group produced an alternative travelogue on Ethiopia, and on images of dereliction in Southampton, using tape and slides. These materials were disseminated to other schools. Eleven schools developed a project on India, and all schools worked on the topic 'Food'. Active learning ideas from the Language Book (ILEA English Centre) also proved popular.

In-Service The project worker organized day conferences for teachers in 1986 and 1987 in conjunction with other advisory teachers and the Head of the Professional Centre. In March 1987, 10 sessions were held for head teachers on: involvement in multicultural education, winter festivals, children's books, drama, learning from photographs, issues in GCSE geography, prejudice, and development issues.

Comments and Effects The new activities were popular with pupils, possibly due to the active learning techniques involved. The teachers found the work enriching, some became enthusiastic and other advisors gave time to 'thinking the issues through'. The project deliberately kept a low profile but the worker sometimes found the strain of keeping it going 'intolerable'. The lack of a LEA policy on multicultural education was considered to be unhelpful.

Kirklees
Name: Multicultural Advisory Team (to support initiatives in countering racial harassment)
Duration: April 1985 – 88
Staff: Three full-time workers, expanded to 20 led by the advisory teacher for 'Education For All' and organized into

Funding: ESG for three staff, LEA funding for the rest
Location: Multicultural centre
Coverage: 10 middle and 30 secondary schools, and two further education colleges. Initially, they worked in 10 pilot schools

four teams covering primary, secondary, languages, and curriculum development

Background   Kirklees is a multi-ethnic area with some 10 per cent ethnic minority people. The authority has a history of positive policies towards the education of minority pupils and wished to respond to the Swann Committee by working in white schools to provide an appropriate 'Education For All'. The ESG project was intended to create a team to support initiatives in countering racial harassment, which was perceived to be a problem in the area, but was only a part of other initiatives in the LEA. All schools had replied to a directive from the Chief Education Officer in July 1986, that they develop plans to implement policies of 'Education For All' and it was on the agenda for all governing bodies.

Aims   To promote education for a multiracial society; to combat racism; to raise teacher expectations of pupil performance; to support working parties and curriculum change.

Methods   The teams visited the schools and helped to set up working parties, a resource centre was established, serviced by the project workers, and materials were made available for schools.

Materials and Pupil Programmes   Middle school projects included names and naming systems, friends and bullying, and 'faces' via the arts and crafts curriculum at secondary level. Multicultural work was developed in dance, music and drama, and some anti-racist science teaching was introduced.

In-Service   This was the major priority for the project and the LEA allocated two days of in-service time per teacher. By 1987 over two thousand teachers had participated. In-service days were organized around 'An Introduction to Multicultural Issues'. Work included an examination of textbooks and library books, workshops on teachers' classroom behaviour, designing a 'subtly racist' school and teaching anti-racism in personal and social education.

Comments and Effects   Positive effects included the enthusiasm of many teachers, favourable written reports, and widespread knowledge of the existence and work of the project team. Negative effects included the indifference and hostility of a few teachers. From 1987 the team was very much aware of the controversy in Dewsbury about the Headfield primary school – a school with a high proportion of Asians to which 22 white parents were refusing to send their children (see chapter two).

Waltham Forest

Name: Pilot project in schools with a significant number of ethnic minority pupils

Duration: September 1986–July 1989

Staff: One full time secondary level worker from April 1987, one primary worker from April 1987

Funding: ESG

Location: Multicultural Development Service Centre

Coverage: Four secondary schools in the white northern area of the borough

Background The borough, with 17 per cent pupils of ethnic minority living in the southern area, set up a multicultural development service and adopted a policy for 'Education for a Multicultural Society' in the early 1980s but became concerned that there was no impetus to implement the policy in white schools, despite recorded incidents of racial hostility and growing National Front influence in the area.

Aims To assist schools without a significant number of ethnic minority pupils to implement the LEA policy in every aspect of school and community life; to support curriculum developments; to work with teachers to examine racial attitudes in school; to investigate appropriate responses to racism and ways of promoting racial harmony, and ways of removing bias, stereotyping and discrimination.

Methods Initial meetings were held with heads and deputies from the project school, followed by help in setting up school-based working parties and offering information, resources, and helping the working groups with policy drafting. The project officer also worked in collaboration with individual subject departments, especially English, Humanities, Home Economics, discussed playground racism with pastoral staff, and made presentations to school governors and parent-teacher meetings. On this project the worker felt isolated from other projects and took the initiative in developing an *ESG Network Newsletter* from January 1988.

Materials and Pupil Programmes A language awareness course was developed with the English department, initially conducted in Gujerati, which had a profound impact on white pupils. The course examined language use in the classroom, the borough and around the world, and produced useful language awareness materials, illustrating scripts and texts. A topic on South Africa was developed with a Humanities Department and modifications made to the Home Economics courses in the schools.

In-Service This project did not develop or run specific courses. The work was done on an informal basis at governor and PTA meetings.

Comments and Effects Positive effects on pupils included seeing a black worker in a responsible role, the change of attitudes after the language awareness course, and pupil enjoyment of the work. Teachers appreciated being able to discuss issues they had felt unable to raise, but one teacher was overheard to say 'an outsider was opening a can of worms' and at a PTA meeting someone said 'this is the Borough wasting money'. The worker felt frustrated that the pace of change was slow and felt isolated in his position, despite support from the Multicultural Development Service and the existence of a LEA policy.

North Tyneside

Name:	Establishment of a Multicultural Education Centre and 'Education For All' curriculum development
Duration:	Two projects – one April 1985–March 1988 to establish the centre and one April 1986–March 1989 to begin curriculum development as outreach work from the centre
Staff:	Two full-time advisory teachers (one the Centre Head) and a multilingual assistant
Funding:	ESG
Location:	Multicultural Resource Centre, Newcastle upon Tyne
Coverage:	The projects were intended to work within the context of mainstream education and with all educational establishments in the borough

Background The education officers and elected members of the borough were agreed that an equal opportunities and multicultural policy should be implemented and supported ESG bids to further this work. Research conducted by an advisor in 1986, which reported that of 300 pupils writing on 'Black people', 75 per cent held negative attitudes and 25 per cent were strongly hostile, helped to convince senior officers that there was a need for curriculum development (Mould, 1986).

Aims To develop the curriculum in all schools in a less ethnocentric manner and to encourage respect for other cultures and lifestyles; to promote positive education and action against racism; to support the (relatively few) ethnic minority children in the borough.

Methods The Resource Centre was set up and serviced by the Centre Head, who arranged loans of materials, visits and meetings. Four Section 11 language consultants and the LEA Equal Opportunities Unit became linked to the centre. The curriculum advisory teacher worked in any school that invited him, teaching and planning in collaboration with class teachers, leading school assemblies, addressing staff meetings and promoting school policy to deal with racial incidents.

Materials and Pupil Programmes   Popular topics for which material was been loaned by the centre included the history of immigration, pre-colonial history, the myths of pseudo-science, religious education work, language exercises (including an exercise going through the telephone directory to find 'names you think are not English' – this recorded 30 language groups in an area pupils thought was monolingual).

In-Service   A two-day conference for all headteachers in North Tyneside produced a 100 per cent attendance. Sessions were organized for deputy heads, probationary teachers, and courses for primary and secondary heads on developing school policies. Meetings in schools were supported and the projects formed links with Sunderland Polytechnic, which offered certificated multicultural courses.

Comments and Effects   A record was kept of the use of the centre by schools and they were asked to complete a questionnaire on how useful they had found the centre. Teachers kept records of racial incidents in school and presented them to the governors. Positive effects on pupils were not very evident, there was some opposition from older students and organized racist political activity in the borough. Most teachers and governors responded positively but some teachers were resistant to change. Parents were keen to attend the school festivals and celebrations organized by the projects. The workers felt they worked in a good atmosphere of positive teamwork with support from the LEA.

Staffordshire
Name: Education for Life in a Multi-Ethnic Society
Duration: April 1986–March 1990
Staff: Four full-time staff, the director being Head of the Intercultural Centre at Stoke-on-Trent, and three advisory teachers seconded from the LEA
Funding: ESG
Location: Intercultural Centre, Stoke-on-Trent
Coverage: County-wide
Aims   To establish models of sound policy and good curriculum practice, particularly in all-white schools; to enhance teacher awareness of cultural diversity as a vehicle for social cohesion and mutual enrichment; to help teachers identify and counter racist attitudes and practices; to provide support across the curriculum and make resources available to teachers.

Methods　The project workers were asked to help prepare LEA guidelines and implement the county policy statement. The policy was produced in March 1987 and contained an explicit agenda for action for teachers. For the first year, three workers operated in separate schools, working alongside teachers and setting up working parties. Work began in five Stafford schools on *One World Week 1987* 'Who Gets the Credit?' which drew on resources from the local community, local radio and a West Midlands Arts Group. A 'Festival of Many Cultures' was organized in Newcastle-under-Lyme which included exhibitions, public concerts and work by local minority groups. The workers were asked by the Education Department to support teachers by taking a lead in discussions, reviewing textbooks and library books, advising on the selection of materials, and arranging pupil exchanges between schools.

Materials and Pupil Programmes　The Intercultural Centre at Stoke-on-Trent served as the focus for the development of resources and materials.

In-Service　This project did not run courses directly but concentrated on developing a network of interested teachers, on changing teacher attitudes by informal discussion and working with governors to inform and influence them.

Comments and Effects　The team felt their work had suffered from distorted reports in the local press about their work and there had been some adverse comments from teachers. There was evidence, however, that some white pupils had ceased to view black people as inferior and many teachers accepted that there was a reasonable case for educating all pupils for life in a multicultural society.

North Yorkshire
Name:　　 ESG Multicultural Education Project (School Twinning)
Duration: April 1986–March 1987
Staff:　　 No extra staff. The County Advisor and an assistant Education Officer (paid by the LEA) organized the twinning
Funding:　ESG funding for travel and school exchanges
Location: Education Offices
Coverage: North Yorkshire and Kirklees junior schools

Aims　To organize exchange visits between primary schools in North Yorkshire and Kirkless.

Methods　All primary schools in North Yorkshire and Kirklees were invited to take part and nine pairs of schools participated; the planning and implementation was done by the school staffs. Each pair of schools set its own objectives for one-day visits, preceded by teacher meetings.

The pupils began by writing letters to each other and the visits were based on an aspect of culture – a North Yorkshire group visited a mosque and some Kirklees pupils went to a North Yorkshire farm. Small groups of pupils met on 'neutral' territory at Ingleton in Yorkshire and three pairs of schools arranged a residential period at a North Yorkshire centre which allowed the children to live together for several days.

In-Service   After each visit, the teachers held a one-day review conference and found the experience of working with teachers from another LEA extremely valuable. The North Riding College developed a programme of 20-day courses for North Yorkshire teachers, and 33 secondary teachers attended two courses on 'Raising Awareness of Multicultural Issues'.

Comments and Effects   The main positive effects were that pupil and teacher awareness of living in a multicultural society had heightened and teachers were far more knowledgeable about the problems of offering an appropriate non-racist education to white children. There were some problems with the exchanges, including feelings of bewilderment and vulnerability by the inner city Kirklees pupils on their country visits and some irritation by the host children that the visitors had found cows so interesting! Parents were apprehensive initially but eventually there was evidence of clear support from them and from governors and local authority staff.

Cleveland
Name: Advisory teacher for multicultural education
Duration: September 1986 –March 1988 (the worker left in December 1987 and was not replaced)
Staff: One full-time advisory teacher (with an interest in World Studies)
Funding: ESG
Location: Multicultural Centre, Middlesborough
Coverage: All all-white primary schools

Background   A Multicultural Centre had been established in this mainly white area in 1979, and a subsequent county policy statement was concerned with white schools and an appropriate education for all pupils. The authority bid for an advisory teacher to further this work.

Aims   To raise teacher awareness of issues involved in anti-racist, multicultural education in all schools; to offer teacher support; to develop teaching materials and strategies for the 8–13 age range.

Methods   The worker undertook support teaching in all-white junior schools and advised and assisted teachers in their choice of curriculum materials. Cooperation with the social studies advisor was important to the work.

Materials and Pupil Programmes New materials included the development of games linking world issues to British issues, particularly a 'World Feast Game' with instructions on videotape. Self-esteem exercises for pupils and cooperative learning strategies for teachers were developed, and new ways of mapping the world explored. The materials remained at the Multicultural Centre on completion of the project.

In-Service Racism-awareness services were organized at the Teachers' Centre, with the help of a black colleague. The aim was to help teachers feel that it was their professional responsibility to recognize and oppose racism. Courses were organized on a 'World Studies' theme, and a course run jointly with the Centre for Global Education at York University. The project worker also contributed to in-school, in-service courses, and to a follow-up to a Theatre-in-Education project 'Do You Really See Me?', in 20 primary and secondary schools.

Comments and Effects A minority of teachers felt that 'too much was being made of the issues' and the project had to overcome some apathy and competing curriculum demands. Overall the worker felt the effects were positive. The pupils gained self-esteem and teachers had found the racism awareness courses useful and appreciated the collaborative teaching, contacts between schools and resources at the Multicultural Centre.

Warwickshire
Name: Education For All, Curriculum Development, INSET and
              School Twinning
Duration: January1987–89
Staff: Two full-time advisory teachers
Funding: ESG but with LEA commitment to continue the project
Location: Primary school, Stratford-on-Avon
Coverage: Eight primary and three secondary schools

Background An intercultural education policy was initiated by the intercultural advisor in 1985 with support from the Chief Education Officer. The ESG project became one of four Intercultural Support Service Units covering all the county. The policy guidelines assert that 'Warwickshire County Council is committed to the achievement of a democratic pluralist society and recognises the vital role of the education service in working towards this aim. . . . Racism in any shape or form has no place in this society' (Warwickshire LEA, 1987).

Aims To encourage whole-school cross-curricular approaches to multicultural education, especially in white schools; to encourage headteachers to act as supporters and facilitators of curriculum change; to change the attitudes of teachers, governors and pupils and encourage interest and genuine understanding of intercultural work.

Methods Heads who had initially attended a 20-day in-service course were invited to have their schools take part in the project. Eight primary and three secondary schools agreed, including Stratford Girls Grammar School whose Chairman of Governors is also a Governor of the National Shakespeare Theatre. Although based in Stratford, the project team equipped a mobile unit containing curriculum materials and resources and drove round the project schools in South Warwickshire. The schools decided on their own activities and sought advice on permeating the curriculum or developing topics with an intercultural perspective. The grammar school held a Caribbean Focus week and took work on art, music and home economics out to three primary schools. One secondary school chose to work directly on racism and prejudice via personal and social education. One primary school used Indian dance and Hindu culture as a focus for work in mathematics and music, involving parents and the community. Other schools organized visits to inner-city schools, multi-faith visits and intercultural conferences. The project was filmed for the *Education Programme* (BBC TV, 17.3.88) and a description of some of the work published by the Senior Advisor (Sharma, 1987).

Materials and Pupil Programes Each school developed its own programmes, described in the annual evaluation reports to DES. New materials developed were added to the resources in the mobile unit.

In-Service Twenty-day courses for senior staff were held at Warwick University in 1987 and 1988, and a 'cascade' model of in-service planned, with teachers who had attended the courses leading other sessions for colleagues in school. An 'information exchange' through discussions of working parties, advisors and advisory teachers was developed, and the local authority committed itself to keeping the in-service programme funded.

Comments and Effects The intercultural advisor's view was that this project enabled pupils to learn about cultural diversity in Britain, take a broader global view, and develop knowledge of, and more positive attitudes to, people of different races and religions. The grammar school pupils interviewed for the television programme demonstrated sophisticated thinking about problems of race, culture and world issues. Positive effects on teachers included a broadening of outlook, the development of support networks, and new professional contacts and collaboration. Some parental hostility and ignorance of issues by school governors had to be overcome. An external evaluation of this project was done by staff at Warwick University.

Humberside
Name: Intercultural Links Project (with Bradford)
Duration: September 1985–July 1988
Staff: The Director was the Humberside language and drama advisor. Over 30 staff were involved in the exchange project, who were permanent mainstream teachers
Funding: ESG funds for travel, in-service and joint conferences
Location: Humberside Education Office
Coverage: The project dated back to 1982 when two 8–13 year middle schools in Humberside and Bradford were twinned to exchange ideas and pupil visits. The ESG expanded the project to cover 30 classes, mainly 8–13, but with several infant and lower secondary classes involved.

Aims The aims were designated intercultural, language, and personal and social. The intercultural aims were to help children share ideas and experiences as equals; to recognize and counter prejudiced and racist attitudes; to provide opportunities for inter-ethnic friendships. The language aims were to encourage a variety of modes of communication in a 'real' situation and involve children in work which involved talk, writing, planning and decision making. The personal and social aims were to encourage positive images and respect for others; to develop self-esteem in all children by providing learning situations which require cooperation and collaboration.

Methods In all schools, language development was the major focus using a range of multi-media and audio-visual material. For example, pupils exchanged booklets of photographs and photo diaries, as well as letters and reports, between individuals and groups. A joint humanities progamme was developed between schools, and teacher and pupil visits carefully planned. Guidelines on exchange visits were formulated for the LEA.

Materials and Pupil Programmes Oral and written language programmes were produced, focussing on a common piece of literature (*The Railway Children* by E. Nesbitt was popular), slide-tape shows were made, and presentation days of models, drama and photography were organized.

In-Service An induction course for teachers joining the scheme was organized, with mid and end-of-year conferences and a three-day 'writing up' conference for all project teachers. A joint authority course was held in the first year.

Comments and Effects Evaluation was a major focus of the in-service programme and HMI took a particular interest in this linked project. Teachers felt it had positive effects on language development and attitudinal change. However, while individual children formed friendships, white pupils did not necessarily change their attitude to 'Asians' as a group. There was some hostility from white members of the public in Hull to Asian children visiting the city, and occasionally a link between schools was abandoned when their philosophies proved to be incompatible.

Northamptonshire
Name: Teacher training to meet educational needs in a multi-ethnic society
Duration: September 1986 –July 1989
Staff: One lecturer in multicultural education at Nene College and one seconded teacher-fellow
Funding: ESG funds for the teacher-fellow and part of the lecturer's salary
Location: Nene College of Higher Education, Northamptonshire
Coverage: College initial and teacher in-service training

Aims   To contribute to initial and in-service training in multicultural education in college; to provide resources and help implement county policy.
Methods   The lecturer interviewed prospective students, gave lectures and seminars and supervised probationers and students on teaching practice. The teacher-fellow purchased and developed resources, made video tapes of 'good practice' in the classroom, evaluated books in the college library, helped train community language teachers, and joined the existing LEA multicultural team. Both organized in-service courses for primary headteachers.
In-Service   The aim of the primary headteachers course was to create confidence and ability to work well in schools with or without minority pupils. The course included an introduction to the concepts and principles of multicultural education, understanding the experiences of ethnic minority pupils, the pedagogy of multicultural teaching, and the management of change. Headteachers' relationships with parents were particularly explored as several heads had parents who objected to their children 'mixing with gypsies and black people'.
Comments and Effects   The team judged the in-service work to be successful. Headteachers had valued the course, taken the opportunity to exchange ideas and felt in a better position to influence parents. On the negative side, the initial teacher training input did not permeate the whole course.

Derbyshire
Name: Education for All in a Pluralist Society
Duration: January 1986 –89

Staff: One full-time coordinator, a curriculum development officer and a clerical assistant with graphic skills
Funding: ESG
Location: Matlock Education Centre
Coverage: Ten all-white secondary schools

Background   Derbyshire set up a Multicultural Education Support Service in 1982 and a working group of elected members to develop a LEA multicultural policy in 1985. In January 1987, the Council issued a comprehensive action programme *Towards the 1990s* (Derbyshire County Council, 1987) which included a draft statement on 'A Derbyshire approach to Education for all in a pluralist society'. Public consultative meetings were held in 1987 and the policy was eventually adopted. The Local Authority was also involved in a programme with the Institute of Education, London University, on 'Post-Swann curriculum developments' and obtained ESG for a second project, twinning primary schools in Derby. This LEA was particularly committed to a focus on both educational needs of minority pupils and to facing the challenge of curriculum development in white schools.

Aims   To support the work of all-white secondary schools by encouraging the development of an appropriate curriculum; to assist in developing multicultural and anti-racist teaching strategies.

Methods and In-Service   Ten schools, out of a possible 63, were selected with the help of secondary advisors, and strategies for working with the schools developed. A contract was produced covering the mutual commitment (which included collaborative teaching) by the project and the school (see *Appendix 3*). The curriculum development officer then joined the staff of three schools part-time for two terms. The coordinator liaised with the senior management of the all-white schools, developed and organized in-school, in-service training and courses with other advisors and established a large resource centre for curriculum materials at Matlock.

Comments and Effects   The curriculum development work appeared to have a positive effect on pupils' and teachers' awareness of multicultural and anti-racist issues across the country. School working parties formed and whole-school policies were discussed. There was some hostility, however, from a few teachers and pupils. The work has been described by Chauhan (1988).

Newcastle upon Tyne
Name: Education for a Multicultural Society
Duration: Started 1986, continuing
Staff: Advisory staff and 30 teachers

Funding: Newcastle was refused ESG in 1985 and 1986 and decided to fund the project, paying the advisors from mainstream funds

Location: Education Offices

Coverage: All schools in Newcastle upon Tyne

Background The city produced a racial equality policy statement in 1986 and the Director of Education was committed to the view that 'Multicultural education . . . should be an integral part of the educational experience of all young people irrespective of their racial background, . . . a major challenge is to raise teacher awareness and Newcastle has a comprehensive programme of in-service training on strategies for recognising and combatting racism, which will eventually encompass all teaching staff in the city' (Davies, 1988). The project became part of the general initiative to prepare pupils for life in a multicultural society and provide anti-racist education.

Aims To encourage all schools to respond to racist incidents; to review all books and learning materials; to provide in-service training in phases.

Methods A reporting procedure to document racial incidents in schools was developed from 1986, advisory teachers visiting those schools which reported such incidents to offer support and advice. National Front activity in schools was taken particularly seriously, but incidents of name-calling, racist graffiti and racial fights were also recorded.

In-Service A series of three-day courses on 'Strategies for combatting racism' was held, in phases, for advisory support teams, headteachers, senior staff, and staff from nursery, primary, secondary and further education. A teacher's pack was sent to each school with suggestions for one-day, in-school courses. The pack contained a 'summary of race relations in twentieth century Britain', definitions of multicultural and anti-racist education, and articles from the journal *Multicultural Teaching.*

Comments and Effects The in-service courses were evaluated as part of the authority's in-service training, and their effect on teachers found to be mainly positive. Some teachers initially thought that children were being singled out, and books censored, and there was some critical press coverage, but all the teachers' unions and other professional associations supported the racial equality policies. Teachers felt that pupils were learning that certain behaviour was unacceptable in schools but that activities and behaviour outside school were less affected.

Oldham
Name: Project on Racial Harmony
Duration: Started September 1987, continuing
Staff: One full-time
Funding: LEA then ESG from 1988
Location: Multicultural Education and Language Centre, Oldham
Coverage: One white primary school

Background   The authority has a significant number of ethnic minority pupils and a well established Multicultural and Language Centre with a highly professional staff. The Head of a primary school approached the Centre, concerned at the racial hostility exhibited by white pupils and their parents on the council estate served by his school. The LEA wrote bids for a project on Racial Harmony, which were rejected in 1985 and 1986, but were funded from 1988.

Aims   To encourage an atmosphere in which racial differences could be discussed and accepted; to counter negative expectations of other races and cultures; to influence parents.

Methods and Materials   The project worker spent time team-teaching in one primary school, and developing new materials. Activity packs developed at the Centre were used, particularly a foundation project with the theme 'People around us' which covered work in mathematics, language, history and geography. The project joined in work which had been in progress for two years in other all-white schools.

In-Service   Well organized in-service activities at the Centre covered courses for teachers in schools with minorities and white schools.

Comments and Effects   A monitoring and evaluation form was produced by the Head of the Centre and teaching, contacts and meetings relating to the project were recorded. The project was not well received by the parents and from 1988 was merged into a wider Authority initiative. The Head of the Multicultural Service produced a most useful check list entitled 'What is Education for a Multicultural Society?' (see *Appendix 4*).

East Sussex
Name: Education for All. Curriculum development and INSET
Duration: 1987–89
Staff: One full-time advisory teacher
Funding: ESG
Location: East Sussex Professional Centre
Coverage: Throughout the authority

Aims   To identify ways of moving multicultural education forward in East Sussex; to raise teacher interest and awareness; to inform parents of the existence of an LEA multicultural policy and discuss issues.

Methods and In-Service   The advisory teacher went into selected schools to encourage teachers to develop working groups and to find structured ways of developing multicultural education. Working groups were also set up to produce in-service packages which could be used for training in school. Consultation meetings were organized with parents. Some were opposed to any change: 'It's a Christian country' 'We should teach British culture', but overall the meetings were considered useful.

Comments   The ESG project provided an impetus for discussion and analysis of issues with teachers and parents, and for disseminating the county policy. The project worker felt that a 'moderate approach' had to be taken in this area as a confrontational model would not be productive. The emphasis had been on asking what kind of education was appropriate for all children in modern Britain.

Hertfordshire
Name: Curriculum Development in Religious Education
Duration: 1986 – 87
Staff: Two full-time seconded teachers for four terms and a primary advisor from 1986
Funding: ESG then LEA funds for the primary advisor
Location: Hatfield Polytechnic then Hemel Hempstead Teachers Centre
Coverage: 23 schools (17 primary, 1 middle and 5 secondary)

Aims   To advance and support the teaching of multi-faith religious education by setting up a data base for teachers, listing local religious communities, books and resources; to run in-service courses on world religious; to help teachers plan their own courses; to improve the existing RE Centre.

Methods   The project workers contacted over 450 Hertfordshire faith communities and invited them to register with the project and become involved in the teaching of religious education. The project schools were invited to visit a selection of churches, mosques, temples and synagogues. They also helped to devise and implement a multi-faith syllabus, particularly where there were teachers with little training in multifaith RE. An 'Approach to Christianity' as a world religion was developed. Schools were enabled to update and develop multifaith resources and a data base was devised and computerized.

In-Service   The project workers had an input to sixth forms, HMI and general conferences on multicultural education in Hertfordshire. They ran GCSE training days with an emphasis on using local faith communities as a resource, and organized exhibitions of work from the project schools.

Comments and Effects   The team thought the impact 'had been immense, there had been heightened sensitivity to the importance of multi-faith RE and increased cooperation among those involved in RE and those involved in multicultural education'. The resources produced, and the data base of faith communities, were of lasting benefit to the LEA. There were some negative reactions from parents – one objected to his child visiting a mosque, and one Muslim parent wanted his child taught Christianity – but overall the parental response was positive.

Kent
Name: Multicultural resources centre
Duration: 1985–86
Staff: The work was coordinated by the existing Head of the Resources Centre
Funding: ESG
Location: Gravesend, Kent
Coverage: The grant was divided among a series of small projects to allow the Centre to increase its activities

Aims   To enable the best possible materials to reach pupils and teachers to encourage an awareness of a multicultural dimension in all aspects of the curriculum.

Projects and Materials   A Chatham secondary school bought and used materials on festivals and world religions, and a festival of Sikhisms was held at another school. A 'Roots' project at primary schools in the Fort Luton area examined family history, food and leisure, and books for a sociology course on the origins of the family were bought for a Rochester school. A Punjabi dance group was organized by parents at three primary schools and the group was later invited to perform at the Commonwealth Arts Festival in Edinburgh. Nursery-nurse conferences were organized in 1986, and a gypsy play was performed in several schools on the initiative of the advisory teacher for Traveller Education. These, and other projects, brought multicultural activity into white schools which had previously had no contact with the Multicultural Education Centre.

In-Service   Conferences were organized for home, and language, tutors and a Kent Association for Mother-tongue Teaching was formed.

Comments and Effects   The Centre Director reported to DES at the end of this one-year project that the ESG funding had produced a three-fold increase in the centre resources and had encouraged teachers to participate in the selection of materials and in thinking through multicultural issues in the curriculum. In particular there was more discussion in schools which had previously considered multi-cultural education to have no relevance for them.

Croydon
Name: Education for a Multicultural Society
Duration: 1985–88
Staff: Two full-time primary support staff, one secondary support teacher and a senior advisory teacher was appointed as project manager
Funding: ESG for the support staff
Location: Multicultural Centre, Croydon
Coverage: 42 primary and 5 secondary schools

Aims To provide short term in-service training in schools with few or no ethnic minority pupils; to identify and take action on overt and covert racism in schools.

Methods The project manager arranged the placement of staff in selected schools as curriculum development teachers, and the support staff produced a model for the development of their project. The team decided to 'start from the level of awareness of individual teachers' and saw themselves as catalysts who would help staff in schools to meet the requirements of the local authority anti-racist policy. They identified overt and covert racism among pupils and helped staff to devise strategies to overcome it. Some examples of overt racism were: white pupils refusing to hold hands with minority pupils, or not choosing them for teams because 'they smelled'; mimicking intonation patterns; racist graffiti and National Front stickers. Covert racism was displayed in the lack of materials for teachers and pupils, classroom displays which did not reflect minorities, and staff at the swimming pool stereotyping minority pupil behaviour.

Materials The secondary worker produced a science package *Tanz-Tech*, designed to combat stereotypes of developing countries, and *Guidelines for the School Library*. The primary workers collected boxes of materials to be placed in staffrooms, took assemblies and arranged displays.

Comments and Effects The team kept open diaries of the work, teachers completed evaluation sheets and a sample of headteachers and deputies was interviewed. The response to the project was then written up into a full report (Collins, Curran and Draper, 1988). Heads were particularly pleased with curriculum developments in Maths, the Humanities and Music. Teachers were impressed that the project team had been sensitive and 'not rammed ideas down our throats'. Several schools began to develop whole-school, anti-racist policies.

Access to Information on Multicultural Education Resources
(AIMER) – Bulmershe College, Berkshire

This project, based at Bulmershe College of Higher Education, had been set up in 1983 with a grant from the Commission for Racial Equality. From April 1987 the Department of Education and Science provided a three-year grant to continue the project. The aim was to provide teachers and other professionals in education and the social services with information about multicultural resources by:

☐ making contact with LEAs and obtaining copies of relevant resources;
☐ cataloguing and indexing them and listing them in databases;
☐ providing a postal enquiry service offering computer print-outs of resources.

Enquiries for information can be requested listing age range, curriculum theme, geographical areas and specific enquiries. Some of the ESG projects have sent information and examples of their own materials to AIMER, and although by no means a comprehensive service, it does provide a national centre for teacher information in multicultural and anti-racist education.

This chapter has provided a description of the work of a sample of ESG projects on education for a multi-ethnic society. The next chapter offers a brief analysis of these developments and records the views of some of the project workers on the successes and failures of their projects.

Notes

1 The staff employed on the projects described themselves as 'project workers' and most were experienced teachers paid at the advisory level.

Appendix 1 to Chapter 6

Questions for discussion at headteachers meeting

1 How do you introduce a child from another school into your school?
   . . . a travelling child
   . . . a 'minority' religion
   . . . a handicapped child
2 What sort of children are likely to be rejected by others in school?
3 How are prejudice and rejection shown?
4 How do we as a school tackle this prejudice and rejection?
5 How much does any rejection relate to children's strong sense of a local identity?
6 To what extent should we foster a sense of local identity?

7   There have been a number of reports from Cumbrian schools of black adults being well received while visiting in a professional capacity but being abused when walking across the playground. What would be your responsibility as a teacher in this situation?

8   In September, a pupil in a Cumbrian secondary school refused to go into a room with a 'Paki' teacher. In what ways may we, as primary school teachers, have contributed to this situation?

9   What do you think of the media's presentation of different groups in Britain? For example, groups based on class, gender, race, northern/southern regions, etc.

10   Does your school support or challenge media images?

11   Why should prejudice and racism be central concerns for every school in Cumbria?

12   Is prejudice unprofessional for teachers?

13   What sort of INSET would help you and your staff to look at these issues?

Source: Cumbria In-Service Questions

Appendix 2 to Chapter 6

In-Service Training For Primary/Secondary Teachers In 'All-White' Areas

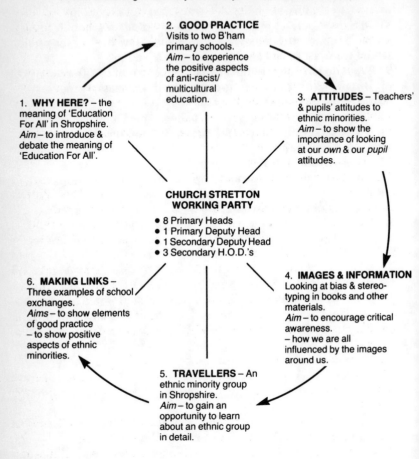

1. **WHY HERE?** – the meaning of 'Education For All' in Shropshire. *Aim* – to introduce & debate the meaning of 'Education For All'.

2. **GOOD PRACTICE** Visits to two B'ham primary schools. *Aim* – to experience the positive aspects of anti-racist/ multicultural education.

3. **ATTITUDES** – Teachers' & pupils' attitudes to ethnic minorities. *Aim* – to show the importance of looking at our *own* & our *pupil* attitudes.

CHURCH STRETTON WORKING PARTY
- 8 Primary Heads
- 1 Primary Deputy Head
- 1 Secondary Deputy Head
- 3 Secondary H.O.D.'s

6. **MAKING LINKS** – Three examples of school exchanges. *Aims* – to show elements of good practice – to show positive aspects of ethnic minorities.

4. **IMAGES & INFORMATION** Looking at bias & stereotyping in books and other materials. *Aim* – to encourage critical awareness. – how we are all influenced by the images around us.

5. **TRAVELLERS** – An ethnic minority group in Shropshire. *Aim* – to gain an opportunity to learn about an ethnic group in detail.

Source: Shropshire ESG Project, 1987.

Appendix 3 to Chapter 6
Derbyshire
The Project Team's commitment to the school
Given the nature of the work being undertaken and the demands from other schools we anticipate being involved with your school for no more than two terms. The Project started in January 1986 and is scheduled to end in August 1988.

Time commitment to the school

1   At the moment the Curriculum Development Officer (CDO) will work in a school for an agreed number of days each week, probably 2 or 3. Occasionally, the Project Team may request that the CDO be released from school (for instance, to provide a session at another school's INSET course) but as far as possible this type of 'disruption' will be kept to a minimum.

2   It is important that the presence of two teachers in the classroom should not be interpreted as making one of them available for 'cover'. The CDO should, however, have the appropriate 'non-contact' time as it applies on a daily basis.

3   The CDO will attend normal staff meetings, is available to undertake 'duties' and is, of course, responsible to the Head of the school when at school.

The school's commitment to the Project Team

Although the situation may vary from school to school the Project Team anticipates the following norms of school commitment:

1   The school would prepare itself appropriately, all staff would be made fully aware of the role of the CDO and fully aware of the Head's support of the Project Teams work.

2   When appropriate, access would be made available to relevant senior staff and to organizational, curricular and pastoral meetings.

3   When whole-school INSET takes place all staff would be invited to attend. The Project Team realizes the difficulties which may arise in ancillary staff participating but the Head is encouraged to involve them as much as possible.

Conclusion of the project team's work in a school

The Project Team will withdraw formally from a school after a period of two terms. By the time the Project Team withdraws it is hoped the school will:

1   continue 'on-going' curriculum development across all subject areas to meet the needs of all for life in a pluralist society;

2   continue regular INSET to raise staff awareness about Education for All in a Pluralist Society;

3   have a formal and explicit policy on anti-racism with mechanisms to monitor and evaluate such a policy.

4   have some members of staff who would be prepared to do limited INSET in neighbouring schools.

The Project Team and the Authority's Advisory Service would, however, offer the appropriate support and advice to the school after the formal withdrawal of the Project Team in order that initiatives established may be further developed.

Source: Derbyshire ESG project, 1987.

Appendix 4 to Chapter 6
What is Education for a Multicultural Society?

Multicultural Education is not . . .	Multicultural Education is . . .
not separate education	is Good Education with all the richness of its implications
not Remedial Education	is education which is appropriate for the child's needs, experience, background etc
not just about language	
not Special Education	
not just another Subject on the timetable	is education which is appropriate for Multicultural Britain
not optional	is education with a wide, indeed a global perspective
not just for black children	
not easy	is main-stream education
not a burden provided one has appropriate resources	is cross-curricular
not the same in every school	is about Cultures
not possible without ONGOING Staff Development	is about Racism
	is about Attitude Awareness
	is vital, vibrant and living
	is for *all* children and of benefit
	is of interest to all teachers
	is of interest to parents
	is of interest to the Community in its broadest sense

Source: Produced by S. Bourne, Head of Multi-Cultural and Language Service, Oldham.

7 An analysis of project work

This chapter provides an analysis of the aims, methods of working, in-service work, and perceived effects of the ESG projects described in the previous chapter and includes comments made by the project staff, both during interviews and at the three ESG Conferences organized in 1987 and 1988.

An important initial point is that the ESG projects reported here, and those in progress around the country, are based in areas that are controlled predominantly by Conservative local councils. Of the projects described, 15 were located in areas which, in 1987, were Conservative, two where there was no overall political majority, and six in Labour controlled areas. The image created by the 'popular' press in Britain in the 1980s, reinforced by right-wing writings (Palmer, 1986a and 1986b; Lewis, 1988), is that multicultural and anti- or non-racist education is a left-wing activity confined to Labour controlled councils and areas. This is simply untrue. These projects demonstrate activity all around the country and there is a growing awareness among elected councillors of all parties that some aspects of the education system need to change to take account of the changing nature of British society and Britain's role in the world. The projects have been recognized as an appropriate way to start making curriculum changes, and to influence pupil, teacher and parent attitudes in white areas. However, despite different political allegiances, those LEA officers and advisers who wrote bids for projects, and those experienced teachers who were appointed as project staff, shared similar views about the need to challenge racial injustice and inequality in Britain, and they shared the belief that this must be done by educating the next generation of young people in a more appropriate fashion.

Aims

A DES requirement was that the aims of all projects should be clearly articulated and achievable. This was intended to minimize rhetoric and ensure that projects were not deflected by pressure groups and other external influences. Inevitably, a measure of rhetoric was apparent in some of the project aims – 'raising awareness', 'challenging', 'promoting' and 'developing' being statements of intent that are not easily measured. The projects all listed a variety of aims – numbering between one and eight – with some dividing them into long- and short-term. A summary of the long-term aims is shown in Table 1.

Table 1. *Aims of projects in white areas*

Raise awareness of multicultural nature of society/promote education for all in white areas.	20
Challenge/appraise the extent of racism, stereotyping and racial hostility/promote principles of racial justice and equality.	17
Develop curriculum materials/promote curriculum opportunities.	15
Help with pedagogy/strategies/methods.	8
Develop/extend INSET activity in and out of schools.	23
Change teacher attitudes/awareness.	8
Change pupil attitudes.	4
Change/work with parents, governors	4
Foster links between schools/co-ordinate individual work	6
Run/act as a resource centre.	5
Stimulate/extend LEA policy.	3
Foster links with minority communities/organizations.	2

The major aims were concerned with raising awareness of the multicultural and multiracial nature of society, promoting a more appropriate education for all, and countering racism, racial hostility and stereotyping of minorities. In the majority of projects these were dual aims which were not considered mutually exclusive. Aims of 'raising awareness' and 'changing teacher attitudes' were partly shorthand for persuading colleagues that they could be implicitly, if not explicitly, helping to perpetuate inappropriate values in the curriculum. The aims and methods did illustrate that the presentation of 'multicultural' and 'anti-racist' approaches as mutually exclusive (Troyna, 1987) may have been too dogmatic and may have misrepresented the actual situation in schools. There was little evidence of the multicultural tokenism which some writers have suggested is characteristic of multicultural education. Rather, the ESG projects indicated that curriculum methods, materials and approaches which offered accurate knowledge about other cultures and ways of life, could also be used to challenge beliefs in white cultural, economic and political superiority.

While aims did not fall neatly into multicultural and anti-racist divisions, they did reflect local needs and priorities. In areas where issues of race and ethnicity had seldom been raised, project staff described their aims as 'starting from where people are', 'taking a softly-softly approach' or 'not frightening colleagues off'. There was general acknowledgement that any confrontational approach was likely to be counter-productive, especially in areas where race was not even perceived to be an issue needing debate or action. In some areas it was easier to attain aims of providing a 'cultural' knowledge-base about minorities in Britain and ways of life in other countries, than to challenge assumptions of racist behaviour and white superiority, although work which could have been described as 'only multicultural' eventually led to the point where entrenched attitudes were being challenged.

Most projects aimed at either the development of curriculum materials or the provision of curriculum opportunities for teachers unfamiliar with the issues, and eight were specifically concerned with strategies and pedagogy – how to 'get the message across'. Eight projects aimed to work directly on teacher attitudes, although opinion was divided on how far such attempts could succeed. One worker thought such attempts were 'pointless' and only a properly enforced LEA and school policy would bring about the necessary changes in behaviour. Six projects aimed specifically at fostering links between schools with high and low proportions of ethnic minorities by twinning or visiting, and these projects appeared to achieve their stated aims. Five projects aimed at running or developing a resource centre although other projects specifically repudiated this as an aim. Developing or extending in-service training was a stated aim of most projects. Three had the aim of developing or extending LEA policy and two aimed to foster links with minority communities.

Although the projects were expected to evaluate their own effectiveness by the achievement of aims, a DES paper conceded that 'It is recognised that measuring progress may be difficult where the ultimate aim is a change in attitudes or practices' (DES, 1987).

Methods of working

Methods of working varied according to the nature and location of the project, but Table 2 is a summary of the methods used in those visited.

Table 2. *Methods of working*

1. In-service activity (see below).
2. Curriculum development, provision of new curriculum opportunities by:
   a. project producing materials/packs/videos;
   b. projects collecting published/duplicated materials;
   c. project acting as a resource centre/data base;
   d. production of materials in collaboration with teachers;
   e. evaluating existing materials.

3.   Demonstration lessons, team and collaborative teaching, taking assemblies.
4.   Advice, guidance, response to requests for help, production of new ideas.
5.   Help in setting up school working parties, talking to or with the whole school staff, departments, individuals, help in twinning arrangements (in-school INSET).
6.   Bringing in outside personnel, especially theatre, drama, art, literary figures and performers/helping with festivals and celebrations.
7.   Approaching governors/parents – parents' workshop, 'packs' for governors.
8.   Monitoring racial incidents/working to produce anti-racist LEA and school policies.
9.   Interviewing in the community/working with religious groups.
10. Research or action research.

The majority of workers were allocated a number of schools to work in, the number varying but not according to the number of project staff. Thus, in one project three workers were assigned to one school while in another, two workers were given eight schools to work in. Some projects concentrated on one age group, others took on an age spread, only two included nursery level, one the further education level and one was located in a teacher training college. Workers generally accepted their allocation but some had more difficulties than others in negotiating access to schools, and becoming fully accepted and supported. One project in particular found that while the headteacher ostensibly supported the work, he contrived to put obstacles in the way of any constructive work.

The two major methods of working were via in-service activity and by curriculum development. Most projects had some involvement in the production of materials for lessons or topics, videos for pupils or of work being done, 'packs' of materials for pupils and teachers, and in one case, a pack for governors. Most projects collected, published or duplicated materials, depending on resources, and some acted as resource centres. Those based in existing multicultural centres could offer a wider range of resources but project workers were adamant that resources did not necessarily change attitudes. The projects also helped teachers to evaluate existing materials, for example, by producing 'guidelines for school libraries'.

Collaborative or team teaching, and demonstration lessons were found to be a most successful method of working, as teachers could then 'see it being done'. Much of the workers' time was taken up with offering advice and guidance and responding to requests from schools for help in setting up working parties, giving lectures or informal talks to school staffs, departments or individuals or leading discussions. Those projects centred around twinning or exchange visits encountered particular problems for staff and pupils in school as well as for the project staff, who were occasionally surprised at the extent of public hostility to the presence of ethnic minority children in white areas.

Projects found that bringing in visitors from the arts, theatre and literature was a very successful strategy which stimulated pupil interest and response. This was most marked where the visitors were non-white, as the drama and literature could provide a vivid illustration of their experiences in a white society. Four projects worked with parents or governors, two running parent workshops, and there was a widespread view that a major task in the future was to find strategies to influence and educate white parents. Two projects worked with religious communities – Catholic, Protestant, other Christian and other faith groups – and three projects specifically engaged in research.

One of the major issues arising from the methods of working concerned pedagogy. Workers felt that the ESG projects had important implications for teaching methodology, and raised questions about the whole teaching-learning process. The most successful and appropriate classroom strategies used by the projects were cooperative and collaborative, both between project staff and teachers, and between pupils. Pupils actually saw project workers and teachers cooperating, discussing multicultural materials, and presenting the work in a mutually acceptable, rational manner. It became obvious that it was impossible to discuss equality, fairness and justice, within an authoritarian, competitive and hierarchical framework of relationships in school and classrooms. Teachers realized that active and interactive learning strategies were crucial and passive learning was often inappropriate, in the context of multicultural and non-racist education.

Project workers felt that many of the difficulties associated with curriculum development were part of a larger general problem of teacher resistance to curriculum change. Some secondary school teachers, for example, held strong beliefs in their 'subject' having a separate and distinct identity, often implicitly based on Eurocentric beliefs, and they found cross-curricular themes, as well as cross-cultural themes, difficult to deal with. One of the most successful curriculum innovations involved the use of World Studies materials. Ten of the ESG projects were based in LEAs which participated in a *World Studies 8–13 Project* set up in 1980 (Hicks, 1987). By 1987, more than half the local authorities in England and Wales used World Studies material in their schools – one attraction being that children found the activities interesting and enjoyable. This material was also used in a number of projects to help teachers present global issues, encourage understanding of minority life experiences in Britain and help pupils form links between their personal world and the wider world.

Pupil programmes

The range of pupil curriculum programmes in the 23 projects is shown in Table 3.

Table 3. *Content of and assistance with pupil programmes*

General

Input into maths/maths trail development/maths work published
Input into language and literature
Input into science, history of science, biology/world science
Input into art, craft technology and design curriculum
Input into humanities, social studies and economics
Input into home economics curriculum
Input into dance, drama, movement
Input into religious education/personal and social education

Specific

Art and culture of other countries – especially Nigeria, India
Poetry and theatre presentations by visitors
Drama workshops
Media education – video production, photography
Music of other countries

World studies
History of immigration
Pre-colonial history
History topic work on India, Australia, Africa, South Africa, the Caribbean

Geography – GCSE development
                        different ways of mapping

Language awareness materials
Languages around the world
Story– black heroes, different people
Multicultural fiction

Harvest/alternatives to harvest festivals
World festivals/One World Week/Sikh festivals
Commonwealth focus

RE work – visits to faith centres
                   multifaith syllabus production

Dance and Movement – Indian dance
                                         – Punjabi dance group
                                         – African drumming

Topic work – food, especially bread
        – houses, animals, names and naming
        – friends and bullying, travellers and their children
        – people around us, nature of prejudice
Non-racist materials – attitude awareness pack
            – Tanz-Tec project
        |– Guidelines for school library
            – Self-esteem exercises
            – Games on world issues
Visits, exchanges to town/country, to farms and faith centres
Special displays e.g. World scientists

The extent of input to the general curriculum and the specific topics or themes developed, demonstrates that it is possible to examine, influence and change whole areas of the curriculum so that pupils are presented with more appropriate, challenging or less biased information and knowledge. Project staff and teachers were very aware of the large amount of work necessary to change even small areas of the curriculum, often because they were consciously devoting time to examining the values and premises underlying the knowledge to be offered to the pupils. For example, one project had developed an Economics Awareness course for third year secondary pupils, centred on an activity called 'The Breakfast Table' (which led into GCSE work). In this, pupils examined the origins of food and packaging, and discussed ways in which countries might produce their food, how they were affected by what they ate, the interdependence of trade in food, and the implications for consumer choice. Another project worked on an alternative presentation of nineteenth century Indian history, examining the events of 1857 from the point of view of British writers (The Indian Mutiny) and of Indian writers (The First War of Independence). In developing new curriculum approaches and materials, project staff and teachers involved became aware of the need to guard against replacing one bias or omission with another, and they constantly faced the issue of whether any knowledge or information could be neutral or value-free.

The way in which curriculum materials were used emerged as more important than the actual content. Topics and lessons *could* remain at the level of passing over seemingly neutral facts or information, and cross-cultural material *could* remain at the level of a 'celebration of diversity'. For example, teachers who had not adequately thought through topic work on food, houses, festivals and religious celebrations could be helping to enhance notions of Western or white superiority. One of the tasks of the project staff was to demonstrate that the same materials could be used to challenge entrenched ideas of cultural, economic and political superiority. Projects on 'Bread', for example, were popular in a number of primary schools, some more successful than others in challenging attitudes. One project worker commented that 'if we can persuade children that the height of civilisation is not embodied in the white sliced loaf we have got somewhere.'

Some of the materials produced were deliberately designed to question received stereotyped ideas. A project on the development of technology in Tanzania sought to impart accurate information and challenge pupils' views of 'primitive Africa'. The staff, however, became very aware that new materials could become an end in themselves – a resource-led activity; as one worker put it, 'Give me a book on Eid, do me a project on India'. They saw their task as moving teachers on to levels where the material could be used to challenge ideas of racial and cultural superiority, which, as described in chapter three, still permeate much of education in Britain. What seemed to be happening in the project schools is illustrated in Table 4.

Table 4. *Levels of change*

Level 0.
    No change/defensiveness/opposition.

Level 1. *Changing the curriculum*
    1(a) curriculum development, resource led activity, ignoring the question of attitudes.
    1(b) curriculum development, materials used to challenge received ideas and change attitudes in a non-racist direction.
    1(c) curriculum development where the content includes direct consideration of bias, stereotyping, prejudice, racism by pupils.

Level 2. *Changing adult attitudes*
    INSET, consultation with parents, governors, and others, curriculum development leading to awareness of the need for whole school policies, and to change in teachers' own attitudes.

Level 3. *Changing practices*
    Development and implementation of equal opportunity, non-racist policies and whole school commitment to changed practice.

Schools which refused to take part in projects, or which dropped out, were presumed to remain on level zero. They were characterized by denials or defensiveness on the level of 'no problem here' or 'you people are just stirring things up'; or by outright opposition to the project work. However, few schools stayed on level zero once a project had begun to make an impact.

In some projects there were problems in developing or using *any* materials which challenged a white, Eurocentric view of the world. The Croydon evaluation report (Collins, Curran and Draper, 1987) details incidents of white pupils responding in a racist manner to topic work, fiction or displays, which included black people, whether they were presented in 'third world' or 'first world' situations. Posters of black people overseas in traditional dress, and of black people in professional situations were equally defaced by racist graffiti. Even world atlases were sometimes defaced in this way and materials which depicted the multi-ethnic nature of society were used as a butt for racist jokes. On one occasion, a display of 20 world scientists, five each of white males and females, and five each of black males and females was considered by a local librarian to be 'unbalanced'.

As many of the projects developed, direct consideration of issues, bias, stereotyping and racism became easier to address. This was taken to be an indication that teachers *had* begun to consider the values underlying curriculum materials and presentation. Project workers thought that a combination of curriculum development, in-service work, and consultation with pupils, parents, governors, local councillors and others, could lead to situations where adult attitudes were changed sufficiently for a general acceptance of non-racist policies and practices in white schools. A few schools had reached what could be described as level 3, where there was support for a whole-school commitment for changed practices, supported by parents and the local community. Actually going through a democratic process of consultation and education of adults involved, and making a genuine commitment to changed practices was, however, very different from simply producing the 'pieces of paper' noted by Davis (1984) and Troyna and Ball (1985).

In-Service work

In-service teacher training was both a major aim and a method of working for all the projects. Workers were unclear at what point helping schools to set up working groups, talking to whole schools or departments, and giving general help and advice ceased to be a normal method of working and justified the title INSET. They were often also unsure on what kind of in-service work was needed in particular situations. As one put it, 'If the ultimate aim is to raise awareness and change attitudes, do I put on a course in new ways of mapping the world, or show a video on racism?' In fact, the projects developed a variety of school-based and out-of-school activities as Table 5 indicates and most projects combined them.

Table 5. *INSET activities*

(organized by project staff and/or advisory groups)
School-based

Working parties, groups, committees – of senior staff, or interested
teachers, of departmental heads, etc.
Whole school meetings, staff meetings
Individual teacher discussions
In-school lectures and discussions, led or given by project staff

Outside school
Head teachers meetings/courses
Senior staff/deputies courses
Regional support groups
Networks between schools
Twilight/evening sessions
One day conferences/courses
Residential conferences/courses
Teachers centres (existing) courses attended
Courses for library/home tutor staff
Courses/workshops with parents
Courses/workshops with governors
Input into college courses
Courses for project teachers at University/College
Joint LEA courses
Courses for project workers

One project set up school-based working parties, arranged half-day
school closures for discussions with staff, and made presentations to
governors and the parent-teacher association. Another had adopted a
cascade model of external courses for headteachers and deputies, who
then organized courses in their schools. Only one project included
arrangements for the project staff to go to courses before and during
their work, although several had links with local polytechnics, colleges
or universities. Sessions held at teachers centres included the following
subjects: race and racism, race awareness, racial behaviour, town and
country, world studies, world education, media awareness, multifaith
activities, multicultural arts, community languages, GCSE input, and
school libraries. For 'awareness' sessions, videos made by John
Twitchin for the BBC in the early 1980s were still used and relevant.
Other videos found useful included *The Black and White Media Show*,
Black, *The Enemy Within*, *Racism*, *The Fourth R* and *Being White*.
The project based at the teacher training college helped supervise
probationary teachers and ran an in-service course for primary
headteachers. In this sample of projects, more primary headteachers
than secondary were involved in these activities.

Effects of projects

The projects visited had been operating for a relatively short time – between two and three years. It was thus difficult to evaluate if attitudes had changed, awareness raised or racial hostility and inequality challenged, although all projects had built in some form of internal evaluation to judge the effects of their work. Table 6 shows the positive and negative effects the workers felt the projects had had on pupils, teachers, parents and LEA personnel.

Table 6. *Positive and negative effects*

Positive effects on pupils
significant pupil enthusiasm for curriculum development
response to new, interesting, challenging work
awareness raised, some attitude changed
more acceptance, awareness of other people
active learning techniques appreciated
drama work had demonstrable effects
good response to black project staff (in relevant projects)
good effects from exchange visits
inter-ethnic friendship in exchange projects
good response to racial behaviour policy (where relevant)
language development benefits
Negative effects on pupils
some racist remarks made on project work
some racist graffiti on curriculum materials
occasional lessons a 'platform for racism'
some pupils influenced by local National Front
some pupils bringing parents'/family negative attitudes
occasional poor response to black workers
some bewilderment on exchange visits
racial behaviour policies less effective outside school
Positive effects on teachers
widespread appreciation, enrichment of professional and personal life
raised awareness, 'it made me think'
new professional skills developed
permeation of curriculum better understood
committed teachers able to pursue ideas
existing initiatives were legitimated
acceptance of relevance of multicultural education
difficulty of work recognized
INSET appreciated, especially whole-school INSET
easier to recruit for external courses
appreciation of contact with project staff
appreciation (by Heads and teachers) of opportunity to exchange ideas, and
   developed contacts
appreciation that materials/resource maximized potential of the work

evaluation sheets/questionnaires on projects favourable (where relevant)
Negative effects on teachers
some alienated, hostile, antagonistic
reluctance to change curriculum
complaints of inadequate resources
defensive reactions, reticence, indifference
some misinformation about project work
some overt racism
'missionary attitudes' of the committed annoyed some teachers
Positive effects on parents
encouraging comments on new work, displays
support for international events, festivals, drama work/poetry sessions
parental interest in multifaith activities
parental support on exchange visits
consultations, discussion with project staff valued
attitude survey of parents (on one project)
'no complaints' counted as a positive effect!
Negative effects on parents
some early apprehension, worried phone calls, about projects
occasionally parent, governor, vicar opposed to project
fundamental Christian objection to some projects
some general antipathy, projects 'wasting money'
Positive effects on other LEA personnel
raised awareness among all advisers
advisers recognition of multicultural, anti-racist dimension
advisory teachers mutual support
awareness at senior office level
support from elected members, and governors
support from section 11 staff
support from DES welcomed, at local level
Negative effects on other LEA personnel
none reported from other officers
occasional local councillor opposition
occasional demonstration of governor ignorance/hostility
Press
some bad publicity in national and local press
some support and good publicity from local press

A table of overall effects, Table 7, indicated that the positive effects outweighed the negative. Given the magnitude of the tasks these projects had been set, which was in effect to change part of the value-base of the whole education system, it was not surprising that negative effects were reported, and it was encouraging that at such an early stage, they were able to report so many positive effects.

Table 7.

	Positive effects	Negative effects
Pupils	11	8
Teachers	14	7
Parents	7	4
Other LEA personnel	7	2
Press	1	1

The response from white colleagues

The project staff found that many of their initial experiences confirmed previous evidence about the views and attitudes of teachers in white areas. Some teachers preferred to deny or minimize the extent to which racial and ethnic tensions were reflected in white schools, and others were over-optimistic, in the face of contradictory evidence about their pupils' level of knowledge about and tolerance of, non-white people in British society. Project workers found that some teachers made statements similar to those found by Matthews and Fallon while researching for the Swann committee (DES, 1985a, p. 244):

- ☐ we have no racial or ethnic minority problems here
- ☐ multicultural education is not relevant to us
- ☐ you are putting ideas into children's heads
- ☐ this is just another bandwagon
- ☐ all this multicultural stuff is going too far the other way
- ☐ blacks and Asians are racists themselves anyway

At the extreme one project worker reported that he had heard arguments from teachers in his area similar to those presented by Lewis, a leader writer on the *Daily Mail*, whose book attacks those employed in the 'race relations industry' as potential revolutionaries bent on social strife (Lewis, 1988, p. 13 and see *ESG Newsletter*, no. 2, 1988). An illustration of teacher denial of their pupils racism was provided by a black project worker who reported that on her first visit to one of her designated schools, a boy announced that 'a spade has arrived'. When this was recounted to the class teacher she insisted that 'none of my pupils could say such a thing'.

The tactics adopted by project workers to persuade hostile or defensive white colleagues of the value of the work were varied and time-consuming. The Cumbria worker aptly dubbed the process 'a struggle for dialogue', and said that the task of pre-empting defensive reactions had not been built into project aims or methodology. Workers quickly realized that in the contentious and emotive area of race relations 'intellectual arguments do not move people'. One strategy to move teachers on from a denial of problems was simply to discuss how attitudes to race *were* emotional and unthinking. Another was to attempt to shock colleagues by presenting them with clear evidence of their pupils racism, although as noted above, some teachers were so defensive on their pupils' behalf, that they refused to accept such evidence. There was clear agreement among project staff that arguing with 'hard-line racist' teachers was pointless. Three workers on one project advised 'back the winners, don't waste time in schools where there is too much hostility, negative feeling or lack of awareness'. Other workers stressed that 'not engaging in fruitless discussion or forcing issues' and 'starting on the teachers' own terms' were good tactics. Project staff felt that one measure of success of their work was their ability to persuade unwilling or luke-warm colleagues of the value of the work, and noted that many teachers who had not previously thought about the issues eventually became committed to the project. The project workers came to regard themselves as facilitators, 'helping others to get things going'.

Another strategy some workers adopted with white colleagues was to arrange a 'linguistic compromise' where they found that media and political presentation of multicultural or anti-racist education as a 'looney left' activity had an effect. Some teachers were reluctant to engage in activities with these labels, but were happy to accept the work simply under the label of 'curriculum development'.

There was a mixed response from white teachers and pupils to black project workers. Of those reported here, six projects employed at least one worker of Asian or Afro-Caribbean origin, and several others sought the assistance of black colleagues, particularly on in-service courses. The workers themselves had mixed feelings. One said 'When I turn up in schools I get the feeling they are thinking – here's that pushy Asian again.' On the other hand, three projects specifically noted the positive effect on pupils of seeing black people in responsible professional roles. Black workers felt frustrated by the slow pace of change and more inclined to 'challenge racism as openly as possible', although one black worker commented 'since what we are doing is undoing three hundred years of history, we can't do it overnight.' Another black worker thought that white project staff were more likely to hear overt racist comments as teachers and pupils were often guarded in their responses to black workers and thought there could be some advantages in having white workers explore white attitudes. White workers also had mixed feelings about their work and relation-ships to white colleagues. One noted that on her project three white women had been appointed and the 'image of white liberals attempting to convert other whites' was strong. She also felt there was a connection between the lack of status afforded to some projects, and the number of women employed.

Project status

Some workers felt, more acutely than others, that their projects had a low status in the LEA, or were not considered particularly important, even by the participating schools. Workers were aware that teachers had many other demands on their time but it was noticeable that enthusiasm often varied in accordance with the support given by headteachers and senior staff. The most successful projects were those which had, in addition to school support, full local authority support from the Chief Education Officer downwards and particularly from local advisers and inspectors. Perceptions of the importance of the work obviously varied among LEAs and senior staff. The Chief Education Officer in Manchester agreed to open the ESG Conference in Manchester in July 1988, but on the day, sent an adviser in his place, whereas the CEO in Warwickshire, who later moved to Newcastle upon Tyne as CEO, was personally very supportive of the projects in both areas.

The short-term nature of the projects and the workers' contracts also affected status. Those projects where there was a local authority commitment to continue the work, and those which formed part of continuing work, were more likely to be regarded as important. Initially, some projects employed staff at the assistant teacher level, but a DES recommendation that all workers be paid on the advisory teacher scale raised their status considerably.

Some projects had clearly defined parameters and a clear brief in terms of time and tasks – for example, the project in the teacher training college, and the school twinning projects. Workers on other projects often felt uncertain where a project began and ended. They often received requests for help from colleagues outside project schools, but were uncertain how much time to devote to schools not in their project brief. Where there were few staff, especially those with only one worker, the feeling was strong that 'we are expected to change the world single-handed.'

Dissemination of information

All projects thought that a lack of dissemination of information between projects while they were in progress had been a serious problem. While the actual working to achieve aims may have been a *process* in which all participants had to be involved, some workers thought 'there was a limit to re-inventing the wheel'. If information about other project strategies and methods had been available, workers felt their own job would have been easier. Four projects, for example, thought that if they had learned about the Derbyshire strategy of negotiating an initial 'contract' with the schools, rather than simply depending on goodwill, they could have more readily gained the cooperation of their own schools. There was some irritation that although the DES laid stress on receiving an annual evaluation report from each project, these were not generally available. Workers felt that the DES should have given more attention to an evaluation of the projects, both on a short and long term basis, so that good practice could be identified and transferred into mainstream work around the country.

In the absence of formal links between projects, workers eventually developed informal networks, particularly on a regional level Three national conferences were held in 1987 and 1988, and the Waltham Forest project initiated a national ESG newsletter from January 1988. The National Anti-Racist Movement in Education (NAME) undertook to disseminate information from projects, and one of the Wiltshire workers became the secretary of NAME. By 1987, some project workers had begun to publish accounts of their work (Sharma, 1987; Chauhan 1988; Brown, 1988a) and workers thought that more articles in practitioners' journals, as well as academic journals, would help to disseminate information.

The 23 projects described in chapter six have, at a conservative estimate, affected the work of some 4000 teachers and there is some evidence that the teachers themselves did not regard them as short-term, one-off events. By 1988, there was the beginning of local and regional teacher networks and teacher support groups. Additionally many local education authorities had accepted that the project work should be incorporated into mainstream education and long-term planning. Not all authorities agreed, however, and some workers thought that after three years of settling in and 'beginning to work for real' the project would close down with no guarantee that the work would be continued or disseminated.

Workers' views of the future

The Education Reform Act became law in 1988 and the proposed changes in the structure, organization and content of education made it a bad year for any forecasts on the future of any aspect of the system. Since the first ESG projects were only just coming to an end in 1988, 25 were continuing and 50 more starting, the future of the work was obviously uncertain. However, the workers did offer some forecasts on the future of their projects.

There was considerable anxiety that multifaith religious education would be affected by the requirement that religious education should 'in the main' be Christian. The workers felt that the wording of the Act did not help parents to distinguish between religious instruction and worship in a particular religion, and religious education which offered all pupils skills in exploring the nature of all religious faith and traditions. Workers generally took the view that multifaith education was an important part of multicultural global education, and were concerned that such a variety of interest groups opposed it. Most workers were optimistic that multicultural and anti-racist work would influence other parts of the national curriculum, since the direction of much work had been curriculum development in specified subject areas.

There was rather more anxiety that the new powers given to governing bodies on finance and budgets could affect multicultural work. Governors who were not sympathetic to its aims were in a position to deflect resources. There was a consensus among workers that future projects should be directed firmly towards governors and parents. There was also anxiety that schools which became 'grant-maintained' and opted out of local authority control, could choose to avoid any multicultural initiatives.

All workers hoped that project work would become part of mainstream education in their Local Education Authorities. How this was to be achieved, however, was problematic. Several workers suggested that the cluster model of schools, developed by the Technical and Vocational Educational Initiative (TVEI) could be adapted, with LEAs clustering schools to work on multicultural materials and ideas. The idea that in future multicultural and anti-racist education could be subsumed under the area of 'equal opportunities' – a suggested cross-curricular theme in the national curriculum – was also popular, although some workers were concerned that the aim of educating white pupils more appropriately could be lost if the focus became equal opportunities for minorities.

Summary

This chapter has offered an analysis of 23 projects described in chapter six, mainly examining workers views of their projects. The projects do illustrate that multicultural and anti-racist initiatives and developments are taking place in selected white schools all around the country, irrespective of party political allegiance in local councils.

The final chapter takes up the question raised in the introduction to this book. Why is there such widespread resistance to the idea that changes are required to make our education system more appropriate for a multi-ethnic society and an interdependent world, and will initiatives such as the ESG projects have any effect in bringing about change?

8 Conclusion

Teachers have to work to readjust humanity's view of humanity: that is the challenge for all-white schools.

(Hussey, 1987)

This book set out to raise questions about the way education can be changed and restructured to reduce tensions and conflicts between groups of young people growing up in an ethnically diverse society. The focus has been on white pupils in white schools, many of whom still leave their schools ignorant about and antagonistic towards non-white people, and reluctant to accept ethnic minorities as their equal fellow citizens. The book has also concentrated on curriculum developments and initiatives in white schools. In the 1980s these schools have been encouraged by both central and local government policies to move away from a 'curriculum appropriate to the imperial past' to one appropriate for a modern interdependent world. This modern world is increasingly being recognized as one in which it makes no social, political or economic sense to assume attitudes of superiority towards those regarded as racially or culturally different, either in Britain or abroad.

Rather than working from the more familiar assumptions in previous literature that the society *is* or *ought* to be regarded as multi-racial, multicultural, multi-ethnic or plural, the emphasis has been on examining the strong opposition to any multicultural, anti-racist educational changes intended to lead to a non-racist society[1] – an opposition which has claimed considerable populist support. An analysis of opposition to *any* developments carrying multicultural or anti-racist labels does make clearer why practitioners attempting to make changes in white areas have experienced difficulties and resistance from colleagues, parents and others.

Opposition and educational nationalism

Some conclusions about the opposition to curriculum changes designed to make education more suitable for an ethnically diverse society can be summarized as follows:

- [ ] Opposition to such changes was relatively muted as long as they were confined to multiracial schools. Once it became apparent, post-Swann, that changes were being advocated in all schools and that white areas would be affected, opposition became more vocal.

- [ ] Opposition has been manifest on two political levels, one a relatively simple party political level by which right-of-centre political capital has been made out of suggesting that all multicultural, anti-racist activities are at best left-wing or at worst likely to be politically subversive. These political attacks have linked multicultural developments to other curriculum areas where children might be encouraged to examine aspects of their society, for example, in World Studies, Sociology or Social Awareness courses, and have purported to be defending educational standards against a mythical multicultural alternative to 'basic subjects'.

- [ ] A more complex political opposition has related to the question of who belongs within a British 'national identity' and whose version of the British heritage and culture should be accepted as an authentic version. Opposition has particularly centred on curriculum changes that attempt to present British imperial history in an alternative manner, and critics have suggested that such changes would 'destroy British culture' to the detriment of British 'patriotic pride' (see chapter one).

- [ ] Opposition by a variety of political figures, academics, parents groups and others has developed into a recognizable conservative ideological orientation described in chapter one as educational nationalism.

Nationalism is itself an ideological construction by which citizens of a national-state are encouraged to believe in a uniform way of life and a version of the national past that marks them out from outsiders (Smith, 1986, p. 134). A case was made out in chapter one that the white British are attempting to sustain an identity created primarily in late Victorian times, assisted by an imperialist curriculum, and that non-white minorities are still excluded from full acceptance as part of the British nation.

Educational nationalism asserts that minorities have complete choice and opportunity to join the British nation and assimilate into a 'British way of life' and that their own intransigence and that of their multicultural supporters hinders the process. Educational nationalism denies evidence of racism and racial discrimination and also denies that there are barriers placed in the way of minorities to achieve educational success, other than those they create for themselves, and it urges colour-blind, monocultural educational policies. Educational nationalists are resistant to making changes to an educational system designed for a white majority and pretend that assimilation is either possible or desired by ethnic minorities. This constitutes a hypocrisy that Dench (1986) has suggested typifies many societies which claim to be democratic but have problems in incorporating ethnic groups successfully.

Educational nationalism also pretends that there is only one possible interpretation of the British heritage and culture, and that its values are unproblematically shared by the white majority. It rejects an alternative view that the past is constantly reinterpreted and that current values usually reflect the interests of the most powerful social groups. The strength of the opposition to multicultural education as 'working against the traditional values of Western society' (Hillgate Group, 1987) and 'encouraging the loss of our British heritage and national pride' (Berkshire County Council, 1987) taken together with the political attacks on multiculturalism and its supporters, suggests that the ideas embodied in multicultural education are regarded as a much greater threat to white politically dominant groups, than supporters of change had ever envisaged.

Opposition to multicultural educational change has undoubtedly led to an increased likelihood of racial and religious segregation in schools. Those white parents seeking to have their children educated away from minority children were given wider parental choice by the 1988 Education Act and could count on support from those 'new right' groups supporting such 'educational apartheid'. Some of these groups have also supported Muslim demands for separate voluntary-aided schooling on the grounds that minority groups also need protection from multicultural education (Naylor, 1988a). In reality, if racial and religious minorities do press for separate schooling, educational nationalists will be delighted that a perceived threat to 'the national heritage' has been removed, but the cost of this may well be a divisive fragmentation of the education system, and ultimately of society.

Education for an ethnically diverse society

In the late 1980s however, it is still government policy that all children and young people should be educated appropriately for life in an ethnically diverse society and an interdependent world. This book has documented one way in which the policy was being translated into action through the work of Education Support Grant-funded projects in white areas. An analysis of a sample of these projects suggested that project aims of raising awareness of the multicultural nature of society, challenging racism and promoting principles of justice and equality in all areas, were slowly being realized and the projects were acting as catalysts and agents for change in white areas. The projects were able to support those teachers and others who genuinely wished to change their practices and attitudes, and the attitudes and beliefs of their pupils. They were having clear and positive effects on teachers, pupils, parents and others in areas where education for an ethnically diverse society had previously been considered unnecessary, if it was considered at all. The ESG project work ran parallel to the efforts of other teachers and educationalists concerned to make appropriate changes in 'subject knowledge', and to the values underlying this knowledge that might help to decrease white pupils levels of misinformation, ignorance, intolerance and attitudes of white superiority.

One most important conclusion to an examination of multicultural, anti-racist developments in ESG project areas was that they were predominantly located in areas controlled by Conservative councils; 15 out of the 23 projects reported in chapter six were in such areas. They had the support of people who held a variety of political allegiances and who were agreed that an education geared to an imperial-colonial past which presented non-white people, their histories and cultures as inferior was an inappropriate education. Multicultural, anti-racist developments in white areas in Britain are emphatically not the creation of left-wing activists.

A national curriculum and a national core-value system?
Chapter four documented the emergence of a national curriculum in which all children will participate during the 1990s. There would seem to be considerable scope in all designated subject areas, and in cross-curricular themes, for ensuring that the curriculum becomes more relevant to a modern multi-ethnic society. The importance of the curriculum will not, however, lie in programmes of study, subject knowledge or assessment targets, but in the values underlying these. Ideally, the values will not be imperialistic, Eurocentric or monocultural, but will be multicultural and global. One value will relate to a belief in an open examination of all knowledge, belief, views and opinions, and all children will be equipped with the skills of critical appraisal needed to undertake such a task. This will undoubtedly not please some educationalists and some parents, from both the majority society and some minority groups. But to accept that 'there are many interpretations of the world, and all children need open-mindedly to examine them' (Brown, 1988b), may be the prerequisite for a truly democratic, tolerant society in which white people abandon their attitudes of superiority or hostility to non-whites.

Chapter two documented some positive attitudes from white pupils who did believe that fair play, tolerance, equal rights and 'fraternalism' should extend to minorities and suggested that teachers could capitalize on these views and educate pupils towards democratic values of equal citizenship and equal respect. Teachers in white schools are now being asked to take on a heavy professional and moral responsibility, in helping to bring about the changes required to 'assimilate all groups into a redefined concept of what it means to live in British society' (DES, 1985a, p. 8).

It may be sensible, however, to end on a more cynical note, given the strength of opposition to multicultural educational changes, and to suggest again that while supporters for such change have usually based their arguments on an egalitarian, moral or human rights arguments, economic arguments concerning the need to accept the trained or skilled labour of ethnic minorities at home, and trade with a largely non-white world, may ultimately prove more powerful in challenging and changing inappropriate white values.

Notes

1   Some opponents of multicultural, anti-racist activities began in 1988 to claim that they were in favour of a non-racist society while simultaneously arguing that British society is not racist (see for example Honeyford, 1988).

Bibliography

AKHTAR, S. and STRONACH, I. (1986), 'They call me blacky – a story of everyday racism in primary schools', *Times Educational Supplement*, 19.9.86, p. 23.

ALLPORT, E. W. (1954), *The Nature of Prejudice* Cambridge, Mass., Addison Wesley.

AM WEEKEND, 8.5.87, *A War of Words*, Manchester.

ARNOLD, T. (1905) Quoted in Rich, P. (1986), *Race and Empire in British Politics*, Cambridge, Cambridge University Press.

ASSISTANT MASTERS AND MISTRESSES ASSOCIATION (AMMA) (1987), *Multi-cultural and Anti-racist Education Today*, an AMMA Statement, London.

ATHERTON, M. A. and LAWRENCE, J. K. (1978), *Chemistry for Today and Tomorrow*, London, John Murray.

BAKER, K. (1987), Foreword to *Encouraging Quality*, Department of Education and Science.

BAKER, K. (1988), *The Faber Book of English History in Verse*, London, Faber & Faber.

BANKS, J. A. & LYNCH, J. (1986), *Multi-cultural Education in Western Societies*, London, Holt, Rinehart & Winston.

BANKS, J. A. (1986), 'Race, Ethnicity and Schooling in the United States' in Banks, J. A. and Lynch, J. (eds.), *Multicultural Education in Western Societies*, London, Holt, Rinehart & Winston.

BBC TV (1987), *Getting to Grips with Racism*, 5 Programmes and Teachers' Book, London, BBC Publications Ltd.

BBC TV (1988), *The Education Programme*, BBC 2, 17.3.88.

BERKSHIRE COUNTY COUNCIL (1987), *Multi-cultural Education Policy Guidelines* (5th draft, August), Slough.

BHAGWATI, J. & RUGGIE, J. (eds.) (1984), *Power, Passion and Purpose: Prospects for North-South Negotiation*, Cambridge, Mass., M. I. T. Press.

BLACK, P. (1987), *Report of the Task Group on Assessment and Testing (TGAT)*, London, Department of Education and Science.

BLAIR, J. (1988), 'Black Child in a White World – A Mother's Perspective' in *Ethnicity and Prejudice in White Highlands Schools: Perspectives 35*, Exeter, University of Exeter.

BLEACH, J. (1984), 'English' in Craft, A. and Bardell, G. (eds.), *Curriculum Opportunities in a Multicultural Society*, London, Harper Educational.

BLUNKETT, D. (1987), 'Facing Up To The New Realities', *Times Educational Supplement*, 25.9.87, p. 4.

BOARD OF EDUCATION (1927), *Handbook of Suggestions for the Consideration of Teachers and Others Concerned with the Work of Public Elementary Schools*, London, Board of Education.

BOLTON, E. (1979), 'Education in a Multi-Racial Society' *Trends in Education*, no. 4, pp. 3–7.

BRANDT, G. (1986), *The Realisation of Anti-racist Teaching*, Sussex, Falmer Press.

BRATTON, J. S. (1981), *The Impact of Victorian Children's Fiction*, Beckenham, Croom Helm.

BRATTON, J. S. (1986), 'Of England, Home and Duty: the image of England in Victorian and Edwardian juvenile fiction' in Mackenzie, J. M. (ed.), *Imperialism and Popular Culture*, Manchester, Manchester University Press.

British Social Attitudes (1984), London, HMSO.

BROWN, C. (1988a), 'The White Highlands: Anti-Racism', *Multicultural Teaching*, vol. 6, no. 2, pp. 38–9.

BROWN, C. (1988b), Letters to the Editor, *Multicultural Teaching*, vol. 7, no. 1, p. 41.

BULLIVANT, B. (1984), *Pluralism, Cultural Maintenance and Evolution*, Avon, Multilingual Matters.

BULLIVANT, B. (1986), 'Multicultural Education in Australia: An Unresolved Debate' in Banks, J. A. and Lynch, J. (eds.), *Multicultural Education in Western Societies*, London, Holt, Rinehart & Winston.

BULLOCK, LORD (1975), *Language Across the Curriculum*, London, HMSO.

BURROUGHS, E. R. (1919), *Tarzan the Untamed*, London, Methuen.

CAMPAIGN FOR REAL EDUCATION (1987), *What is the CRE?*, York, Campaign for Real Education.

CARLYLE, T. (1849), *Occasional Discourse on the Nigger Question: in Critical and Miscellaneous Essays Vol. 4*, London, Chapman & Hall.

CARRINGTON, B. and SHORT, G. (1989), 'Policy or Presentation? The Psychology of Anti-Racist Education', *New Community*, vol. 15, no. 2, pp. 227–40.

CARTER, A. (1985), *Teachers for a Multicultural Society*, London, Longman, For Schools Council Development Committee.

CARTWRIGHT, R. I.(1987), 'No Problems Here: Multicultural Education in the All-White School', *Multicultural Teaching*, vol. 5, no. 2, pp. 10 –12.

CHANCELLOR, V. (1970), *History for Their Masters – Opinion of the English History Textbook*, Bath, Adams and Dark.

CHAUHAN, C. (1988), 'Anti-Racist Education in All-White Areas: A Black Perspective', *Multicultural Teaching*, vol. 6, no. 2, pp. 35–7.

COLENSO, J. W. (1892), *Arithmetic – Designed For The Use Of Schools* (2nd edition), London, Longman Green & Co.

COLLINS, P., CURRAN, A., DRAPER, V. (1988), *Education in/for a Multicultural Society – An Evaluation Report*, Croydon, Croydon Education Authority.

COMMISSION FOR RACIAL EQUALITY (1987), *Learning in Terror*, London, Commission for Racial Equality.

COMMISSION FOR RACIAL EQUALITY (1988), *Parliamentary Report: Notes on Issues of Concern to CRC's and Ethnic Minority Organisations in the Current Legislative Programme. The Education Reform Act 1988*, London, Commission for Racial Equality.

COSWAY, P. and RODNEY, R. (1987), 'Multicultural Fiction in a Suburban School', *Multicultural Teaching*, vol. 5, no. 2, pp. 19–23.

COSWAY, P. (1988), 'An Institutional Racism Checklist for Multi-Ethnic and All-White British Schools', *Multicultural Teaching*, vol. 7, no. 1, pp. 30 –35.

COX, C. (1986), 'From Auschwitz – Yesterday's Racism to GCHQ' in Palmer, F. (ed.), *Anti-racism – An Assault on Education and Value*, London, Sherwood Press.

CRAFT, M. (ed.) (1984), *Education and Cultural Pluralism*, Sussex, Falmer Press.

CRAFT, M. (1986), 'Multicultural Education in the United Kingdom' in Banks, J. A. and Lynch, J. (eds) *Multicultural Education in Western Societies*, London, Holt, Rinehart & Winston.

CRAFT, A. and BARDELL, G. (eds.) (1984), *Curriculum Opportunities in a Multicultural Society*, London, Harper Educational.

CRAFT, A. and KLEIN, G. (1986), *Agenda for Multicultural Teaching*, London, School Curriculum Development Committee.

CROSSMAN, R. (1979), *Diaries of a Cabinet Minister*, London, Hamish Hamilton.

CUMBRIA ESG PROJECT (1988), *Starting With Ourselves – Towards Multicultural Education*, videotape, Cumbria County Council.

CUMBRIA LOCAL EDUCATION AUTHORITY (1987), *Education For Life in a Multicultural Society*, Curriculum Paper no. 14.

DA COSTA, C. (1988), *Ideology and Practice in the Black Supplementary School Movement*, Ph.D. thesis, (unpubl) Guildford, University of Surrey.

DANCE, E. H. (1960), *History the Betrayer – A Study in Bias*, London, Hutchinson.

DANCE, E. H. (1971), *History for a United World*, London, Harrap.

DAVEY, A. (1984), *Learning To Be Prejudiced – Growing Up In Multi-Ethnic Britain*, London, Edward Arnold.

DAVIES, M. (1988), 'Week by Week', *Education*, 26.2.88, p. 151.

DAVIES, G. (1984), 'How Pervasive is White Superiority?', *Education*, 22.6.84, p. 511.

DENCH, G. (1986), *Minorities in An Open Society – Prisoners of Ambivalence*, London, Routledge.

DENT, R. (1988), *Faith of Our Fathers. Roman Catholic Schools in a Multi-Faith Society*, Coventry, City of Coventry Education Department.

DEPARTMENT OF EDUCATION AND SCIENCE (1971), *The Education of Immigrants*, London, HMSO.

DEPARTMENT OF EDUCATION AND SCIENCE (1977), *Education in Schools – A Consultative Document*, London, HMSO.

DEPARTMENT OF EDUCATION AND SCIENCE (1981a), *The School Curriculum*, London, HMSO.

DEPARTMENT OF EDUCATION AND SCIENCE (1981b), *West Indian Children in Our Schools*, Interim Report of the Committee of Enquiry into the Education of Ethnic Minority Children (The Rampton Report), London, HMSO.

DEPARTMENT OF EDUCATION AND SCIENCE (1984), *Initial Teacher Training – Approval of Courses*, Circular 3/84, London, Department of Education and Science.

DEPARTMENT OF EDUCATION AND SCIENCE (1985a), *Education For All*, Report of the Enquiry into the Education of Children from Ethnic Minority Groups (Swann Report), London, HMSO.

DEPARTMENT OF EDUCATION AND SCIENCE (1985b), *Better Schools*, Cmnd. 9469, London, HMSO.

DEPARTMENT OF EDUCATION AND SCIENCE (1985c), *History in the Primary and Secondary Years: An HMI View*, London, HMSO.

DEPARTMENT OF EDUCATION AND SCIENCE (1986), *Local Education Authority Training Grants Scheme 1987/88*, Circular 6/86, London, HMSO.

DEPARTMENT OF EDUCATION AND SCIENCE (1987), *Education Support Grants*, Circular 1/87.

DEPARTMENT OF EDUCATION AND SCIENCE (1988a), *Mathematics for Ages 5–16*, Proposals of the Secretary of State for Education and Science and the Secretary of State for Wales, London, HMSO.

DEPARTMENT OF EDUCATION AND SCIENCE (1988b), *Science for Ages 5–16*, Proposals of the Secretary of State for Education and Science and the Secretary of State for Wales, London, HMSO.

DEPARTMENT OF EDUCATION AND SCIENCE (1988c), *English for Ages 5–16* Proposals of the Secretary of State for Education and Science and the Secretary of State for Wales, London, HMSO.

DERBYSHIRE COUNTY COUNCIL (1987), *Towards the 1990s: An Action Programme by Derbyshire County Council for Education For All People in Derbyshire*, Derbyshire County Council.

DUMMETT, A. (1983), *Portrait of English Racism*, Harmondsworth, Penguin.

DURHAM, M. (1986), 'Far right March For Young Minds', *Times Educational Supplement*, 20.6.86, p. 10.

DYSON, D. (1986), 'Multicultural Approaches to Mathematics' in Arora, R. K. and Duncan, C. G. (eds.) *Multicultural Education – Towards Good Practice*, London, Routledge.

Education Reform Act (1988), London, HMSO.

ESG Newsletter, no. 2 (1988), London, Waltham Forest.

Faith in the City – A Call for Action, Archbishop of Canterbury's Commission, London, Church House Publishing.

FAULKS, S. (1988), 'The Minister and the Muse', *The Independent*, 18.4.88.

FIELD, J. H. (1982), *Towards a Programme of Imperial Life – The British Empire at the turn of the century*, Oxford, Oxford University Press.

FILE, N. (1984), 'History' in Craft, A. and Bardell, G. (eds.), *Curriculum Opportunities in a Multicultural Society*, London, Harper Educational.

FINNEMORE, J. (1902), *Men of Renown – A Concentric Historical Reader*, London, A and C Black Ltd.

FLEMING, I. (1952), 'Pleasant Island', *Spectator*, 4.7.52.

FLEMING, I. (1954), *Live and Let Die*, London, Jonathan Cape.

FREIRE, P. (1971), *Cultural Action For Freedom*, Harmondsworth, Penguin.

GAINE, C. (1987), *No Problem Here: A Practical Approach to Education and 'Race' in White Schools*, London, Hutchinson.

GENERAL SYNOD OF THE CHURCH OF ENGLAND: BOARD OF EDUCATION (1984), *Schools and Multicultural Education. A Discussion Paper*, Memorandum 2/84, London.

GIBSON, E. & SADEQUE, S. (1988), *Education and Ethnic Minorities*, London, The Bow Group.

GILL, D. (1987), *Getting to Grips With Racism*, London, BBC TV.

GILROY, P. (1987), *There Ain't No Black in the Union Jack*, London, Hutchinson.

GIMSON, A. (1988), 'Enoch Powell – Midwife to the Spirit of a Nation', *Independent*, 19.4.88.

GOODSON, I. F. (1983), *School Subjects and Curriculum Change*, Beckenham, Croom Helm.

GOODSON, I. F. and BALL, S. J. (1984), *Defining the Curriculum – Histories and Ethnographies*, London, Falmer Press.

GORDON, P. & KLUG, F. (1986), *New Right. New Racism*, London, Searchlight Publications.

GORDON, P. and LAWTON, D. (1978), *Curriculum Change in the 19th and 20th Centuries*, London, Hodder and Stoughton.

GOULBOURNE, H. (1989), *The Communal Option. Nationalism and Ethnicity in Post-Imperial Britain*, Warwick, Centre for Research in Ethnic Relations, University of Warwick.

HABER, L. (1978), *Black Pioneers of Science and Invention*, New York, Harcourt Brace.

HALL, S. (1988), Invited Lecture to Department of Sociology, University of Lancaster, 17.5.88.

HALSTEAD, M. (1988), *Education, Justice and Cultural Diversity*, Sussex, Falmer Press.

HASTIE, C. (1986), 'History, Race and Propaganda' in Palmer, F. (ed.), *Anti-Racism: An Assault on Education and Value*, Wiltshire, Sherwood Press.

HATCHER, R. (1987), ' "Race" and Education: Two Perspectives for Change' in Troyna, B. (ed.), *Racial Inequality in Education*, London, Tavistock.

HECHTER, M. (1975), *Internal Colonialism*, London, Routledge.

HELM, S. (1988), 'Speech Fired Passionate Views', *Independent*, 18.4.88.

HEMMING, R. (1984), 'Mathematics' in Craft, A. and Bardell, G. (eds.), *Curriculum*

Opportunities in a Multicultural Society, London, Harper Educational.

HEMPEL, S. (1988), 'The Real Consumer Backlash', *Times Educational Supplement*, 29.7.88.

HER MAJESTY'S INSPECTORS (1967), *Towards World History*, Education Pamphlet no. 52, London, Department of Education and Science.

HER MAJESTY'S INSPECTORS (1978), *History: Revised Version. 11–16 Document*, London, Department of Education and Science.

HICKS, D. (1987), *World Studies 8–13*, State of the Project Report, Lancaster, St Martin's College.

HILLGATE GROUP (1986), *Whose Schools? A Radical Manifesto*, London, Hillgate Place.

HILLGATE GROUP (1987), *The Reform of British Education*, London, The Claridge Press.

HISTORICAL ASSOCIATION (1987), *National Debate on History in the Curriculum. 5–16*, London, The Historical Association.

HOME AFFAIRS COMMITTEE (1981), *Racial Disadvantage*, London, HMSO.

HONEYFORD, R. (1982), 'Multi-racial Myths?', *Times Educational Supplement*, 19.11.82.

HONEYFORD, R. (1983), 'Multi-ethnic Intolerance', *The Salisbury Review*, no. 4, June, pp. 12–13.

HONEYFORD, R. (1984), 'Education and Race. An Alternative View' *The Salisbury Review*, no. 6, December, pp. 30–2.

HONEYFORD, R. (1987), 'The Swann Fiasco', *The Salisbury Review*, vol. 5, no. 3, pp. 54–6.

HONEYFORD, R. (1988), *Integration or Disintegration? Towards a Non-Racist Society*, London, The Claridge Press.

HOPKIN, J. (1987), 'Developing a Multi-cultural Anti-racist Policy in a White School', *Multicultural Teaching*, vol. 5, no. 2, pp. 22–4.

HUGHILL, B. (1987), 'Dramatic Steps that Will Carry Britain Forward', *Times Educational Supplement*, 16.10.87.

HUGHILL, B. (1988), '£10m Rise in ESG Funds', *Times Educational Supplement*, 29.4.88.

HUMBERSIDE LOCAL EDUCATION AUTHORITY (1988), *Intercultural Links Guidelines*, Hull, Humberside County Council.

HUMPHRIES, S. (1981), *Hooligans or Rebels*, Oxford, Oxford University Press.

HUSSEY, M. (1987), 'In-Service Work', National Anti-Racist Movement in Education, Conference, held in March, Chichester, Sussex.

ILEA (1983), *Race, Sex and Class*, Inner London Education Authority.

Independent, 18.4.88, p. 5.

Independent, 'Schools Row Blamed for Race Attacks', 2.9.88.

INGLIS, F. (1985), *The Management of Ignorance*, Oxford, Blackwell.

JAMES, A. and JEFFCOATE, R. (1981), *The School in the Multicultural Society*, London, Harper & Row.

JARVIS, F. (1978), Letter to *Times Educational Supplement*, 24.2.78.

JEFFCOATE, R. (1976), 'Curriculum Planning in Multiracial Education', *Educational Research*, vol. 18, no. 8, pp. 192–200.

JEFFCOATE, R. (1979), *Positive Image: Towards a Multicultural Curriculum*, London, Chameleon Books and Writers and Readers Publishing Co.

JEFFCOATE, R. (1984), *Education and Ethnic Minorities*, London, Harper and Row.

JOSEPH, K. (1986), 'Without Prejudice – Education for an ethnically-mixed society' reprinted in *Multicultural Teaching*, vol. 4, no. 3, pp. 6 –8.

KELLY, E. and COHEN, T. (1988), *Racism in Schools: New Research Evidence*, Stoke-on-Trent, Trentham Books.

KINDLEBURGER, C. P. (ed.) (1970), *The International Corporation*, Cambridge, Mass., M.I.T. Press.

KIPLING, R. S. (1899), *Stalky and Co.*, London, Macmillan.

KLEIN, G. (1985), *Reading Into Racism*, London, Routledge.

KLEIN, G. (1986), 'Open letter to Sir Keith', *Multicultural Teaching*, vol. 4, no. 3, pp. 4–5.

LANE, SIR DAVID (1987), 'The Commission for Racial Equality: The First Five Years', *New Community*, vol. 14, nos 1 and 2, pp. 12–16.

LANE, SIR DAVID (1988), *Brent's Development Programme for Racial Equality in Schools – A Report*, London Borough of Brent.

LAWSON-WALTON, J. (1899), 'Imperialism', *Contemporary Review*, no. lxxv.

LAWTON, D. (1975), *Class, Culture and the Curriculum*, London, Routledge Kegan Paul.

LAYTON-HENRY, Z. (ed.) (1986), *Race, Government and Politics in Britain*, London, Macmillan.

LEICESTER, M. (1986), 'Multicultural Curriculum or Anti-Racist Education. Denying The Gulf', *Multicultural Teaching*, vol. 4, no. 2, pp. 4–7.

LEVI, T. (1987), 'Forty Years After: A Memoire', *Multicultural Teaching*, vol. 5, no. 2, pp. 4–5.

LEWIS, R. (1988), *Anti-Racism: a Mania Exposed*, London, Quartet Books.

LITTLE, A. and WILLEY, R. (1981), 'Multi-ethnic Education – The way Forward', Schools Council pamphlet 18, London.

LLOYD, T. O. (1984), *The British Empire 1558–1983*, Oxford, Oxford University Press.

LYNCH, J. (1983), *The Multicultural Curriculum*, London, Batsford.

LYNCH, J. (1987), *Prejudice Reduction at the Schools*, London, Holt, Rhinehart & Winston.

MACKENZIE, J. M. (1984), *Propaganda and Empire – the manipulation of British public opinion 1880–1960*, Manchester, Manchester University Press.

MACKENZIE, J. M. (ed.) (1986), *Imperialism and Popular Culture*, Manchester, Manchester University Press.

MANCHESTER ESG PROJECT (1987), *Inside-Outside: An Evaluation Document*, Manchester City Council.

MANGAN, J. A. (1980), 'Images of Empire in Victorian-Edwardian Public Schools', *Journal of Educational Administration and History*, vol. 12, no. 1.

MANGAN, J. A. (1986), 'The Grit of our Forefathers: invented traditions, propaganda and imperialism' in MacKenzie, J. M. (ed.), *Imperialism and Popular Culture*, Manchester, Manchester University Press.

MASSEY, I. (1987), 'Hampshire Happening: Working Towards Change', *Multicultural Teaching*, vol. 5, no. 2, pp. 6–8.

MCGOWAN, E. (1981), 'Mathematics and Numeracy' in Lynch, J. (ed.), *Teaching in a Multicultural School*, London, Ward Lock.

MCNEAL, J. and ROGERS, M. (1971), *The Multi-Racial School*, Harmondsworth, Penguin.

MIDGELEY, S. (1988), 'Dewsbury School Row Avoidable', *Independent*, 10.12.88.

MILNER, D. (1983), *Children and Race. Ten Years On*, London, Ward Lock Educational.

MINISTRY OF EDUCATION (1963), *English for Immigrants*, London, HMSO.

MISHAN, E. J. (1988), 'What Future for a Multi-Racial Britain? Part 1', *Salisbury Review*, vol. 6, no. 3, pp. 18–22.

MOODLEY, K. A. (1986), 'Canadian Multicultural Education. Promises and Pactices' in *Multicultural Education in Western Societies*, Banks, J. A. and Lynch, J. (eds.), London, Holt, Rinehart & Winston.

MOORHOUSE, G. (1983), *India Britannica*, London, Paladin Books.

MOULD, W. (1986), 'No Rainbow Coalition on Tyneside', *Multicultural Teaching*, vol. 4, no. 3, pp. 9–12.

MULLARD, C. (1982), 'Multi-racial Education in Britain – From Assimilation to Cultural Pluralism' in Tierney, J. (ed.), *Race, Migration and Schooling*, London, Holt, Rinehart & Winston.

MULLARD, C. (1984), *Anti-Racist Education – The Three O's*, London, National Association for Multi-racial Education.

Multi-Cultural Education, vol. 5, no. 2, Spring 1987.

MURRAY, S. (1905), *The Peace of the Anglo-Saxon*, London, Watts & Co.

NASH, I. (1989), 'Baker Opts for a Team of Moderates', *Times Educational Supplement*, 20.1.89.

NATIONAL ANTI-RACIST MOVEMENT IN EDUCATION (NAME) (1987), *Anti-Racist Education in White Areas*, Report of a Conference at Chichester, 14–16 April 1988, Walsall, National Anti-Racist Movement in Education.

NATIONAL CURRICULUM COUNCIL (1988a), *Consultation Report: Mathematics*, York, National Curriculum Council.

NATIONAL CURRICULUM COUNCIL (1988b), *Consultation Report: Science*, York, National Curriculum Council.

NAYLOR, F. (1988a), 'Political Lessons of Dewsbury', *Independent*, 22.12.88.

NAYLOR, F. (1988b), 'Parents' Rights', Letter to *The Teacher*, January.

New Society (1978), 'Race and Teachers: Schools Council Study', 16.2.78.

O'KEEFE, B. (1986), *Faith, Culture and the Dual System. A Comparative Study of Church and County Schools*, Sussex, Falmer Press.

PALMER, F. (ed) (1986a), *Anti-racism. An Assault on Education and Value*, Wiltshire, Sherwood Press.

PALMER, F. (1986b), 'Moral Understanding and the Ethics of Indignation', in Palmer, F. (ed.), *Anti-Racism: An Assault on Education and Value*, Wiltshire, Sherwood Press.

PATTEN, C. (1986), Address to HMI Conference, Buxton, 5.3.86.

PEARCE, S. (1985), *Education and the Multi-Racial Society*, Monday Club Policy Paper no. 1124, May 1985, London.

PEARCE, S. (1986), 'Swann and the Spirit of the Age' in Palmer, F. (ed.), *Anti-Racism. An Assault on Education and Value*, London, Sherwood Press.

RACIAL UNITY (1954), *F. A. Norman papers: Letter to the Colonial Secretary, Alan Lennox-Boyd, from F. A. Norman*, 1.10.54.

REX, J. (1981), *Equality and Opportunity and the Minority Child in British Schools*, Paper presented to conference on the Rampton Report, London, Institute of Education, University of London.

REX, J. (1986), *Race and Ethnicity*, Milton Keynes, The Open University.

REX, J. and TOMLINSON, S. (1979), *Colonial Immigrants in a British City – A Class Analysis*, London, Routledge.

RICH, P. (1986), *Race and Empire in British Politics*, Cambridge, Cambridge University Press.

RICHARDS, K. J. (1983), 'A Contribution to the Multicultural Education Debate', *New Community*, vol. 10, no. 2, pp. 222–5.

RICHARDSON, R. (1988), 'Opposition to Reform and the Need for Transformation – Some Polemical Notes', *Mulicultural Teaching*, vol. 6, no. 2, pp. 4–8.

RICHMOND, P. (1981), 'Choosing a Science Curriculum', in Lynch, J. (ed.), *Teaching in a Multicultural School*, London, Ward Lock.

ROBERTS, A. (1987), 'Multi-culturalism as Anti-racism: Where is the Leadership?', National Union of Teachers, *Education Review*, vol. 1, no. 2, pp. 45–9.

ROBERTS, R. (1971), *The Classic Slum*, Manchester, Manchester University Press.

ROBERTSON, C. (1988), *A Survey of the Multicultural Initiatives in English and Welsh Local Education Authorities since the publication of the Swann Report in March 1985 and their Implementation*, M. A. dissertation (unpubl), University of Lancaster.

ROSE, E. J. B. and ASSOCIATES (1969), *Colour and Citizenship – A Report on British Race Relations*, Oxford, Oxford University Press.

ROY, A. and ST JOHN BROOKS, C. (1987), 'Pass or Fail: Parent power and Baker's Bill', *Sunday Times*, 13.10.87.

RUSHDIE, S. (1982), 'The New Empire Within Britain,' *New Society*, 9.12.82.

Salisbury Review (1987), 'How Should the Teaching of History Begin?', Editorial, vol. 6, no. 2, p. 2.

SAVERY, J. (1987), 'Strictly Anti-Racist on Fantasy Island', *Salisbury Review*, vol. 5, no. 3, pp. 4–6.

SCARMAN, LORD (1982), *The Scarman Report: The Brixton Disorders 10–12th April 1981*, Harmondsworth, Penguin.

SCHOOLS COUNCIL (1981), *Education for a Multiracial Society: Curriculum and Context 5–13*, London, Schools Council.

SCRUTON, R. (1986), 'The Myth of Cultural Relativism' in Palmer, F. (ed.), *Anti-Racism – An Assault on Education and Value*, London, Sherwood Press.

SCRUTON, R., ELLIS-JONES, A. and O'KEEFE, D. (1985), *Education and Indoctrination*, London, Educational Research Centre.

SEATON, N. (1988), 'Distorted Images', *Times Educational Supplement*, 1.7.88.

SEELEY, J. E. (1883), *The Expansion of England*, London, Macmillan & Co.

SELECT COMMITTEE ON RACE RELATIONS AND IMMIGRATION (1973), *Education* (3 vols), London, HMSO.

SHAH, S. (1988), 'What Kind of History?', *Multicultural Teaching*, vol. 6, no. 3, pp. 28–32.

SHARMA, S. (1987), 'Education For All On Wheels – The Inter-Cultural Mobile Unit', *Multicultural Teaching*, vol. 5, no. 2, pp. 13–16.

SILVER, H. (1977), 'Nothing but the Past or Nothing but the Present', *Times Educational Supplement*, 1.7.77.

SIMON, B. (1973), 'Research in the History of Education' in Taylor, W. (ed.), *Research Perspectives in Education*, London, Routledge.

SKIDELSKY, R. (1988), 'History as Social Engineering', *The Independent*, 1.3.88.

SLEETER, C. and GRANT, C. (1987), 'An analysis of Multicultural Education in the United States', *Harvard Educational Review*, vol. 57, no. 4, pp. 221– 43.

SMITH, A. D. (1986), *The Ethnic Origins of Nations*, Oxford, Blackwell.

SMITH, D. J. (1977), *Racial Disadvantage in Britain*, Harmondsworth, Penguin.

SPENCER, D. (1988), 'Trial and Error Approach to Anti-Racist Education', *Times Educational Supplement*, 6.5.88.

ST JOHN-BROOKS, C. (1988), 'Battling to Stop the Hijack of a GCSE Subject' *Sunday Times*, 13.11.88.

STEMBRIDGE, J. (1956), *The World – A General Regional Geography* (2nd edition) London.

Sun 'Enoch Raps Queen: She Must Speak Up More for Whites', 21.1.84.

Sun 2.3.87

Sun 'Odd Boy Out', 3.5.87.

SUPPLE, C. (1986), 'Anti-Racist Teaching in the North-East: A Personal View', *Multicultural Teaching*, vol. 4, no. 3, pp. 16–18.

SURKES, S. (1988), 'Baker Fixes Tough Timetable for New Curriculum Council, *Times Educational Supplement*, 2.9.88.

SUTCLIFFE, J. (1987), 'Reform: Marks out of a Hundred', *Times Educational Supplement*, 19.12.87.

TAYLOR, A. (1988), *Multicultural Education in an All-White School* B.A. Dissertation (unpubl.), University of Lancaster.

TAYLOR, B. (1984a), 'Multicultural Education in a Monocultural Region', *New Community*, vol. 12, no. 1, pp. 1–8

TAYLOR, B.(1984b), 'The Seduction of Tokenism in Multicultural Education', *Multicultural Teaching*, vol. 3, no. 3, pp. 17–19.

TAYLOR, B. (1986), 'Anti-Racist Education in Non-Contact Areas: The Need for a Gentle Approach', *New Community*, vol. 13, no. 2, pp. 177–84.

TAYLOR, W. H. (1987a), 'Anti-Racist Education in Predominantly White Areas', *Journal of Further and Higher Education*, vol. 11, no. 3, pp. 45–8.

taylor, w. h. (1987b), 'Ethnicity and Prejudice in White Highlands Schools', *Perspectives*, no. 35, Exeter, University of Exeter.

THATCHER, M. (1982), Speech to Conservative Rally, Cheltenham, 3.7.82.

THATCHER, M. (1988), Speech to EEC Council of Ministers, Bruges, Belgium.

The Times 'Keeping the Lid on the Inner Cities', 19.11.85.

TOMLINSON, S. (1983), *Ethnic Minorities in British Schools – A Review of the Literature 1960–1982*, London, Heinemann.

TOMLINSON, S. (1984), *Home and School in Multicultural Britain* London, Batsford.

TOMLINSON, S. (1987), 'Towards AD 2000: The Political Context of Multicultural Education', *New Community*, vol. 14, no. 12, pp. 96–104.

TOMLINSON, S. and COULSON, P. (1988), *Descriptive Analysis of a Selection on Education Support Grant Funded Projects in White Areas*, Lancaster, University of Lancaster.

TOWNSEND, H. E. R. and BRITTAN, E. (1973), *Multiracial Education: Need and Innovation*, Schools Council Working Paper, no. 50, London, Evans Methuen.

TROYNA, B. (1982), 'The Ideological and Policy Response to Black Pupils in British Schools' in Hartnell, A. (ed.), *The Social Sciences in Educational Studies*, pp. 127–43, London, Heinemann.

TROYNA, B. (1987), 'Beyond Multiculturalism: Towards the Enactment of Anti-Racist Education in Policy, Provision and Pedagogy', *Oxford Review of Education*, vol. 13, no. 3, pp. 307–20.

TROYNA, B. (1988), 'Anti-Racist Institutions in Education', *Multicultural Teaching*, vol. 6, no. 3, pp. 5–7.

TROYNNA, B. and BALL, W. (1985), 'Views From the Chalk-Face – School Responses to an LEA's Policy on Multicultural Education', *Policy Papers in Ethnic Relations No. 1*, Warwick, Centre for Research in Ethnic Relations, University of Warwick.

TROYNA, B. and SELMAN, L. (1988), *You Poor, You Black, You Ugly and You a Woman: Strategies of change along anti-racist lines in predominantly all-white colleges* (unpubl. report); London, Further Education Unit at the Department of Education and Science.

VANCE, M. (1984), 'Biology' in Craft, A. and Bardell, G. (eds.), *Curriculum Opportunities in a Multicultural Society*, London, Harper Educational.

VICKERS, D. (1986), *Pilot project: Educational needs in a multi-ethnic society*, Wigan, Wigan Local Education Authority.

WALSALL ESG PROJECT (1987), *Asian Names: A Guide To Help People Understand the Naming System of People from the Asian Sub-Continent*, Walsall Education Authority.

WARWICKSHIRE LEA (1987), *Curriculum Guidelines: Inter-Cultural Education For All*, Warwick, Warwickshire Education Authority.

WATTS, S. (1986), 'Science Education for a Multicultural Society' in Arora, R. K. and Duncan, C. G. (eds.), *Multicultural Education: Towards Good Practice*, London, Routledge.

WHITE, N. (1987), 'New Resources for All-White Areas', *Multicultural Teaching*, vol. 5, no. 1, p. 47.

WILLIAMS, M. (1986), 'The Thatcher Generation', *New Society*, vol 75, 21.2.86, pp. 312–15.

WILLIAMS, R. (1965), *The Long Revolution*, London, Pelican Books.

WILLIAMS, R. (1983), *Towards 2000*, Harmondsworth, Penguin.

WILLIS, P. (1977), *Learning to Labour – How Working Class Lads Get Working Class Jobs*, London, Gower.

WILLEY, R. (1984), *Race, Equality and Schools*, London, Methuen.

WILTSHIRE LEA (1988), *Mathematics For All*, Salisbury, Wiltshire County Council.

WILSON, M. (1987), 'Not Racist: We just want an English education for our children', *Derby Trader*, no. 968, 23.10.87.

WORKING PARTY ON CATHOLIC EDUCATION IN A MULTIRACIAL, MULTICULTURAL SOCIETY (1984), *Learning from Diversity – A Challenge for Catholic Education*, London, Catholic Media Office.

WORSTHORNE, P. (23.5.82), Editorial, *The Sunday Telegraph*

WYN-WILLIAMS, I. (1984), 'Chemistry' in Craft, A. and Bardell, G. (eds.), *Curriculum Opportunities in a Multicultural Society*, London, Harper Educational.

YOUNG, BARONESS (1980), Address to a Conference on Education for a Multicultural Society, London, Commission for Radical Equality.

Index